OLD FRENCH FAIRY TALES

Illustrated by
Virginia Frances Sterrett

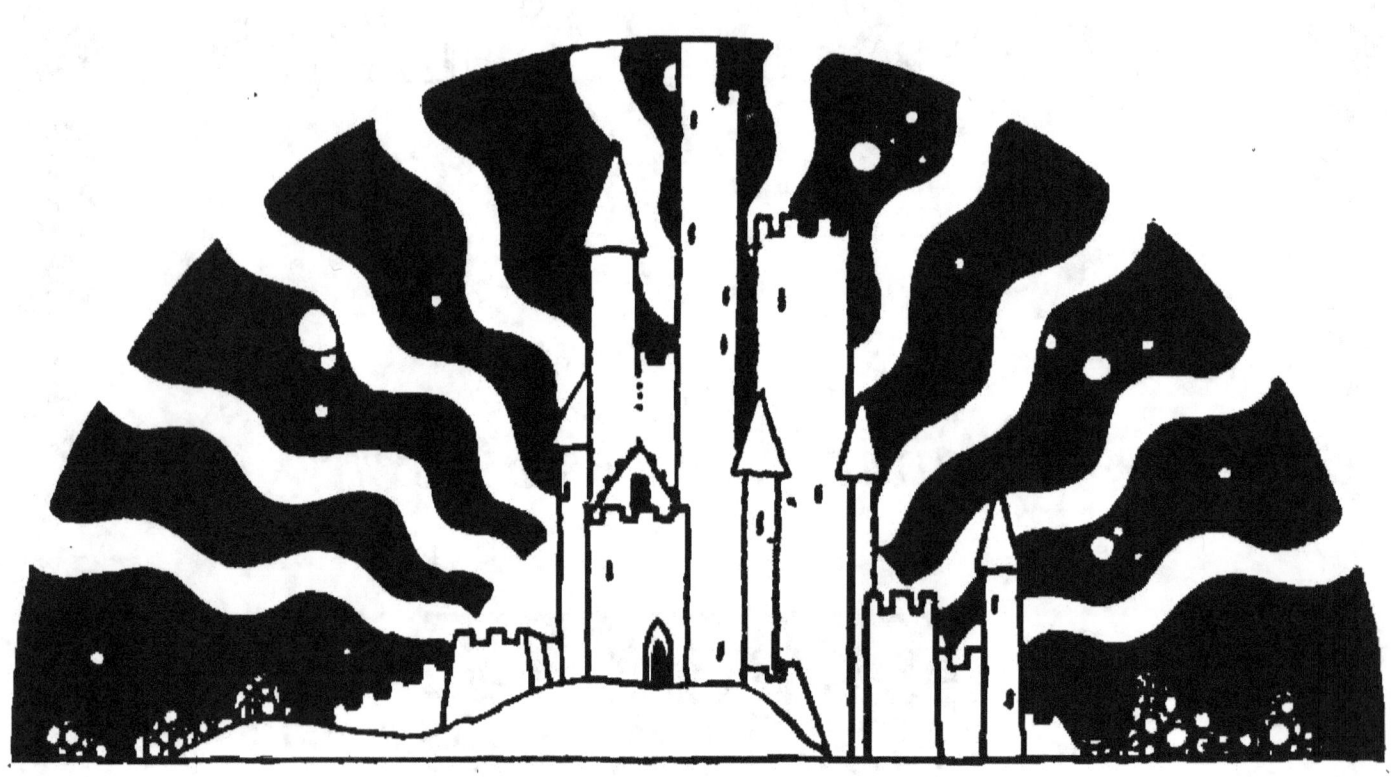

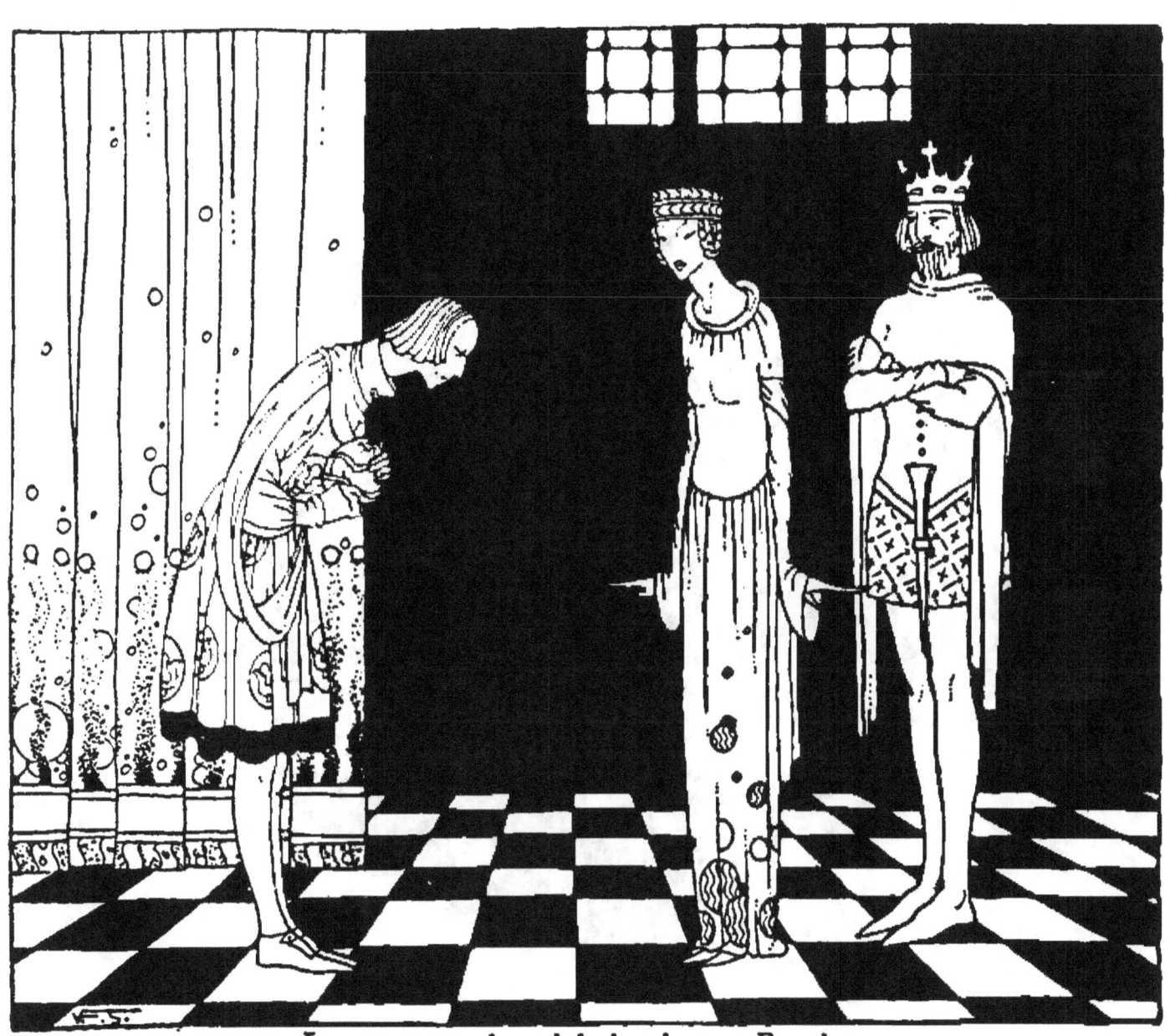

Leger meets the wicked princess, Fourbette

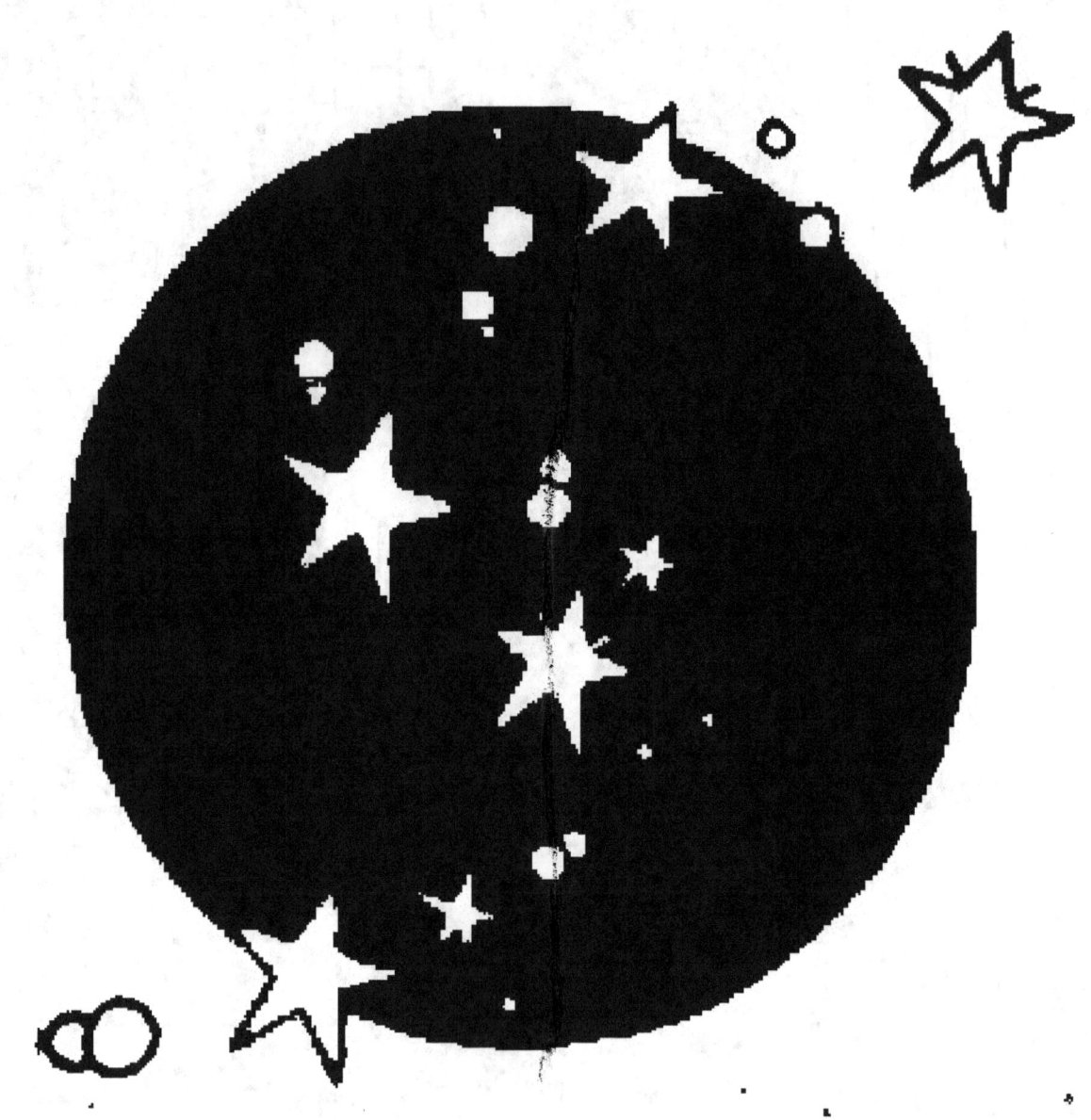

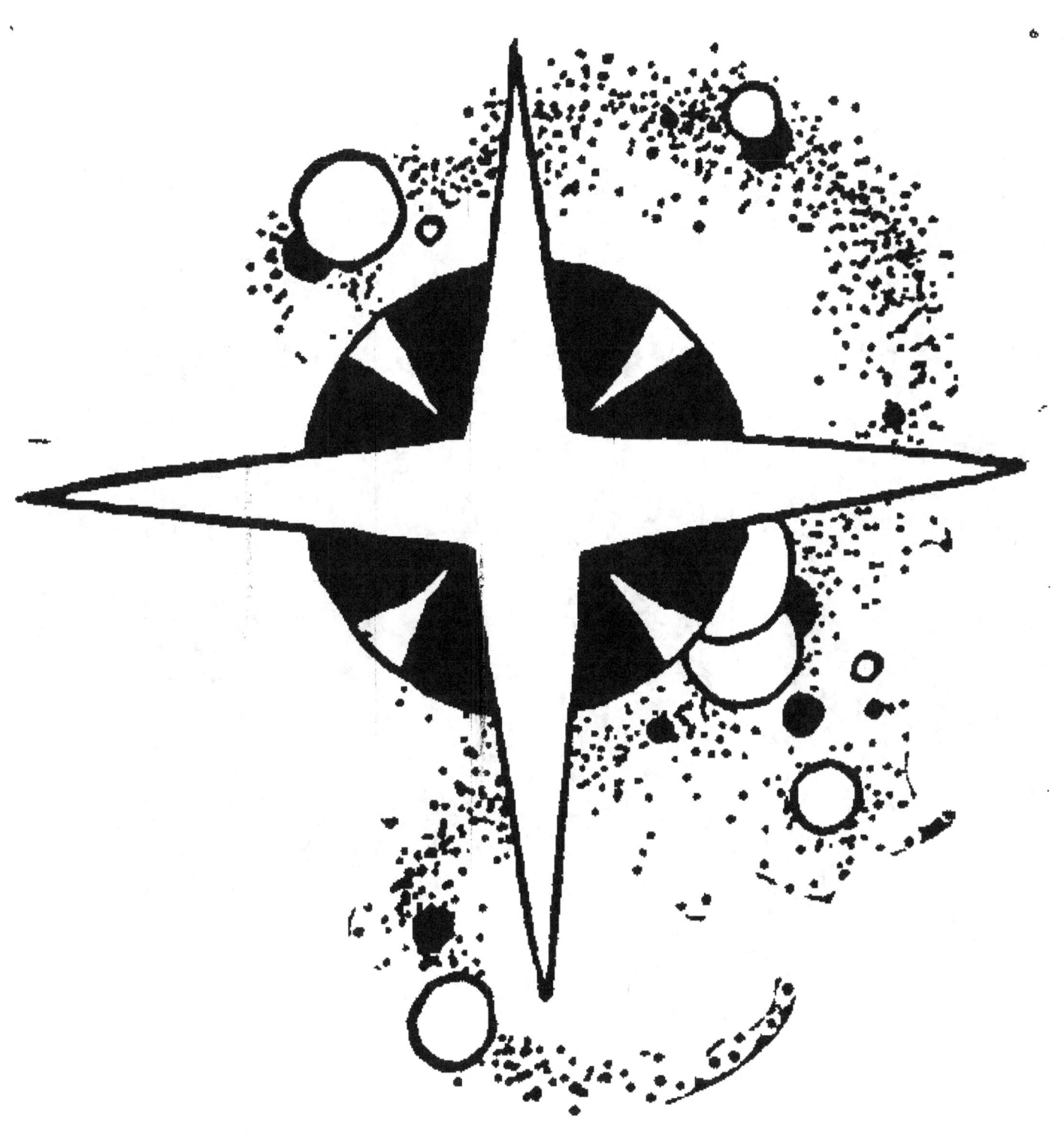

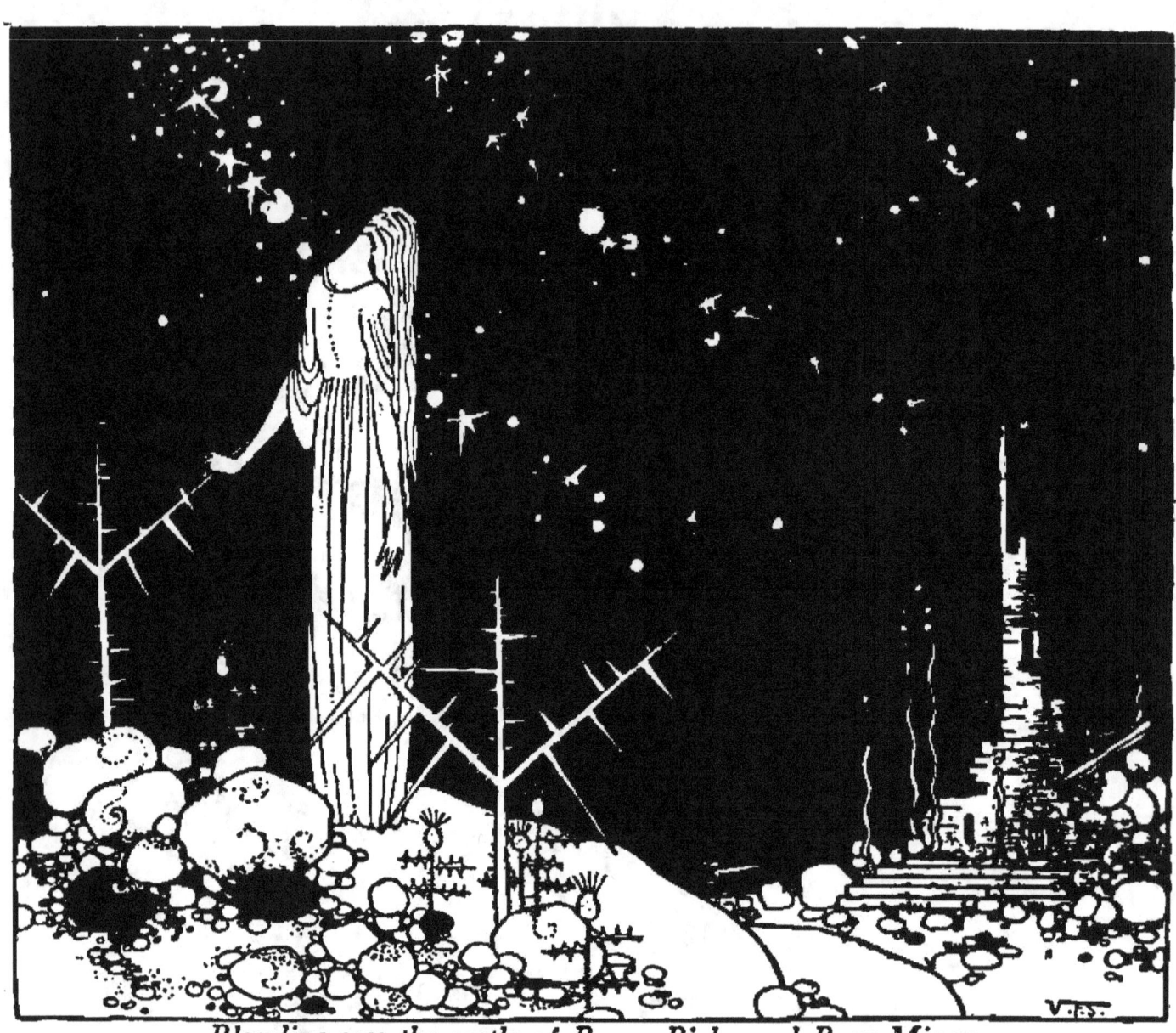
Blondine sees the castle of Bonne-Biche and Beau-Minon

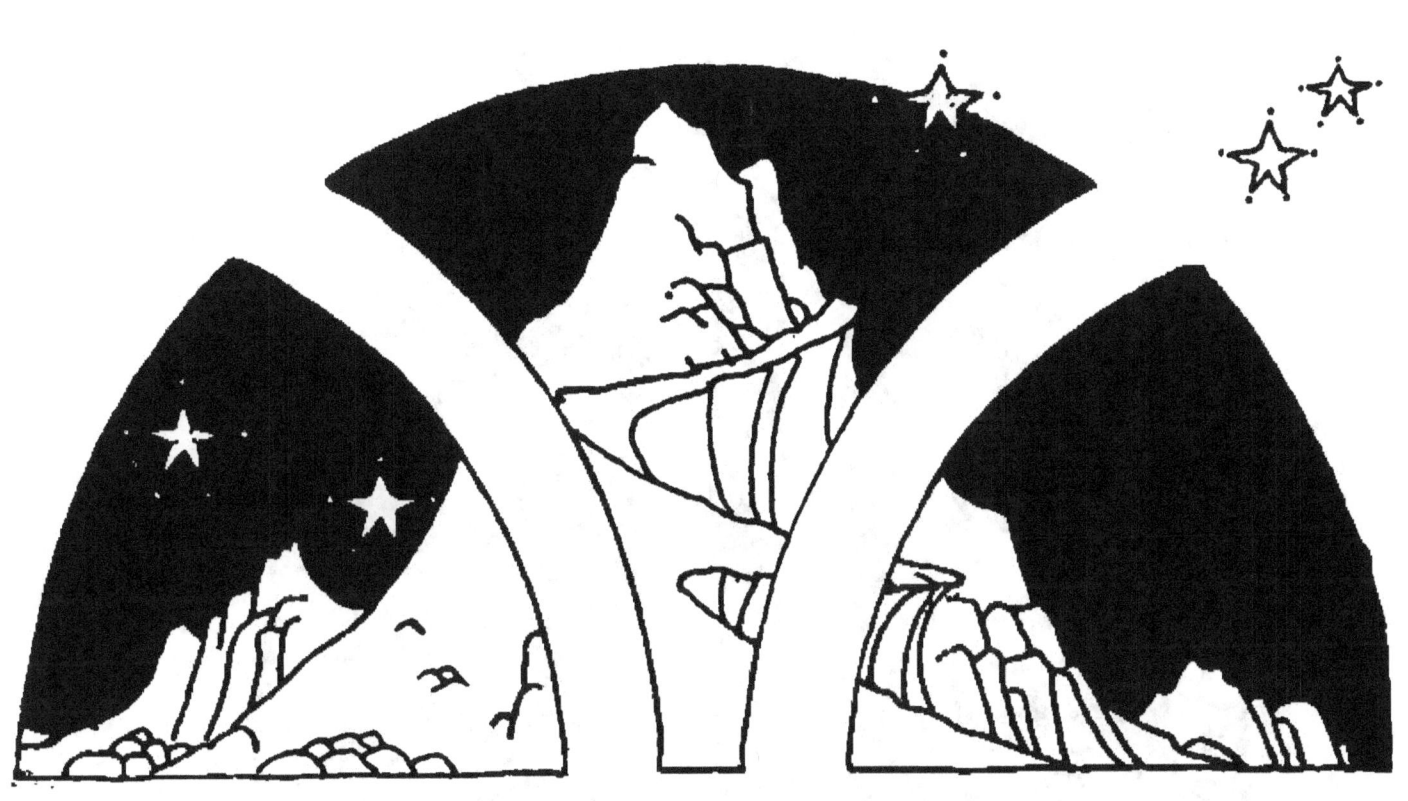

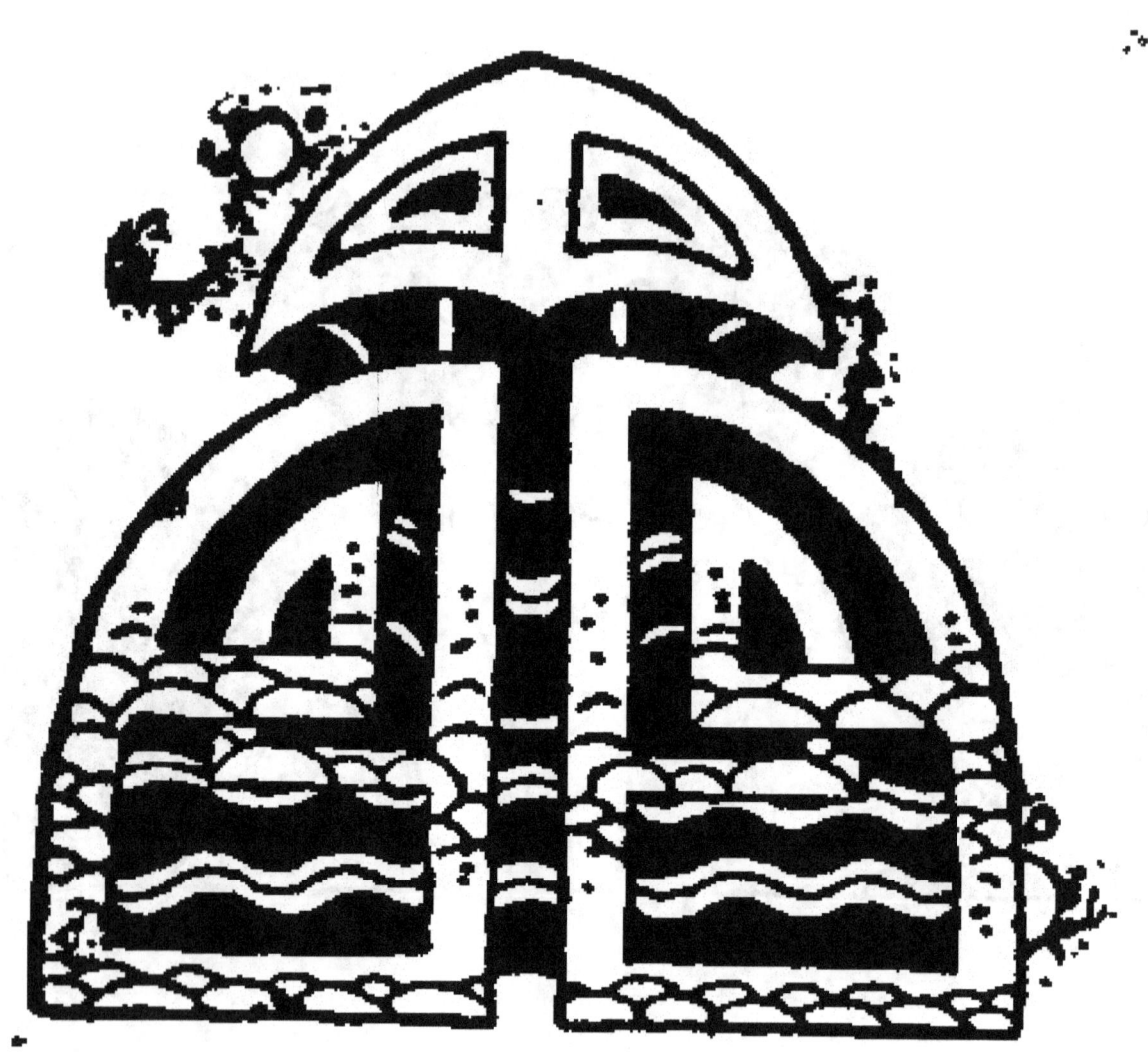

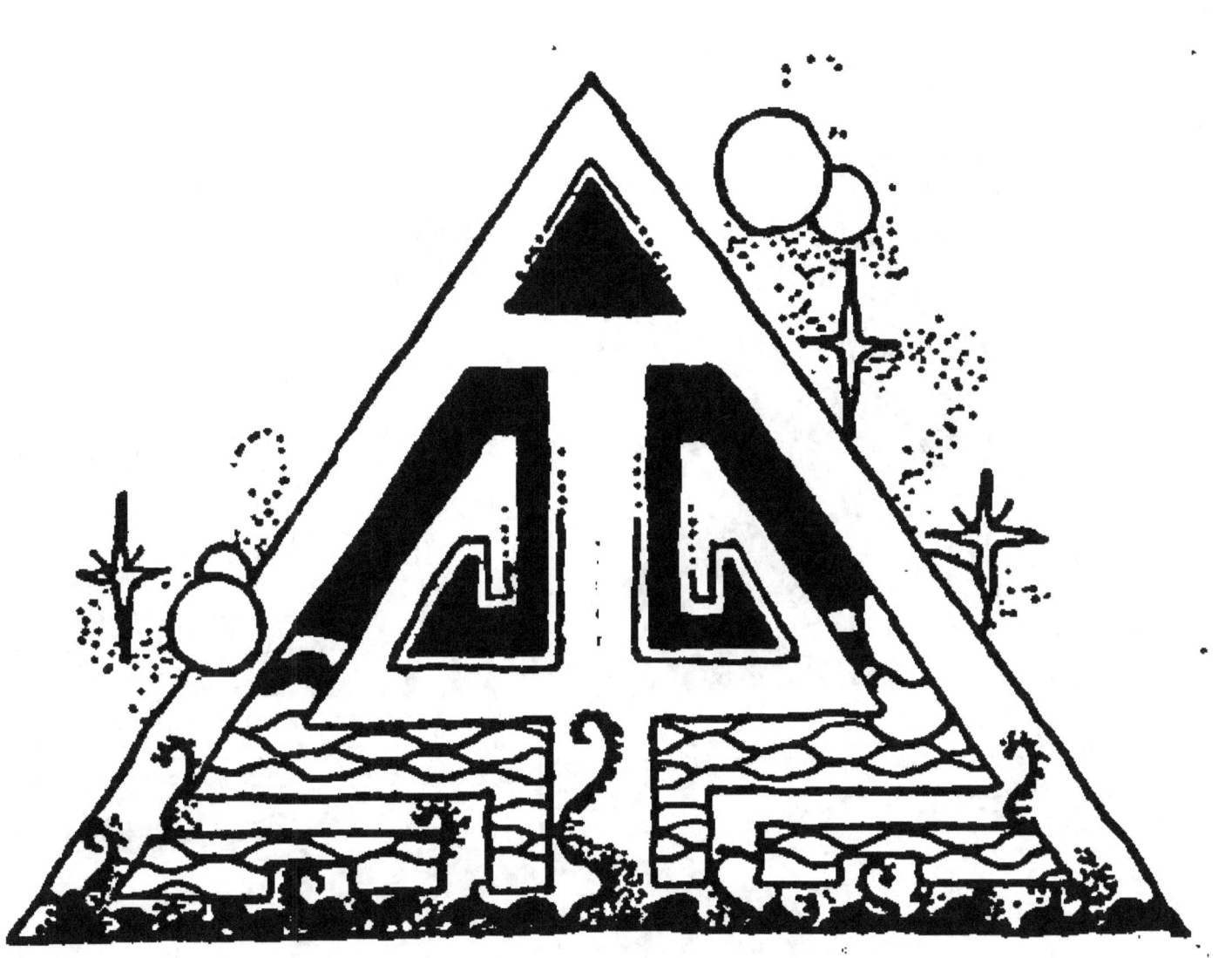

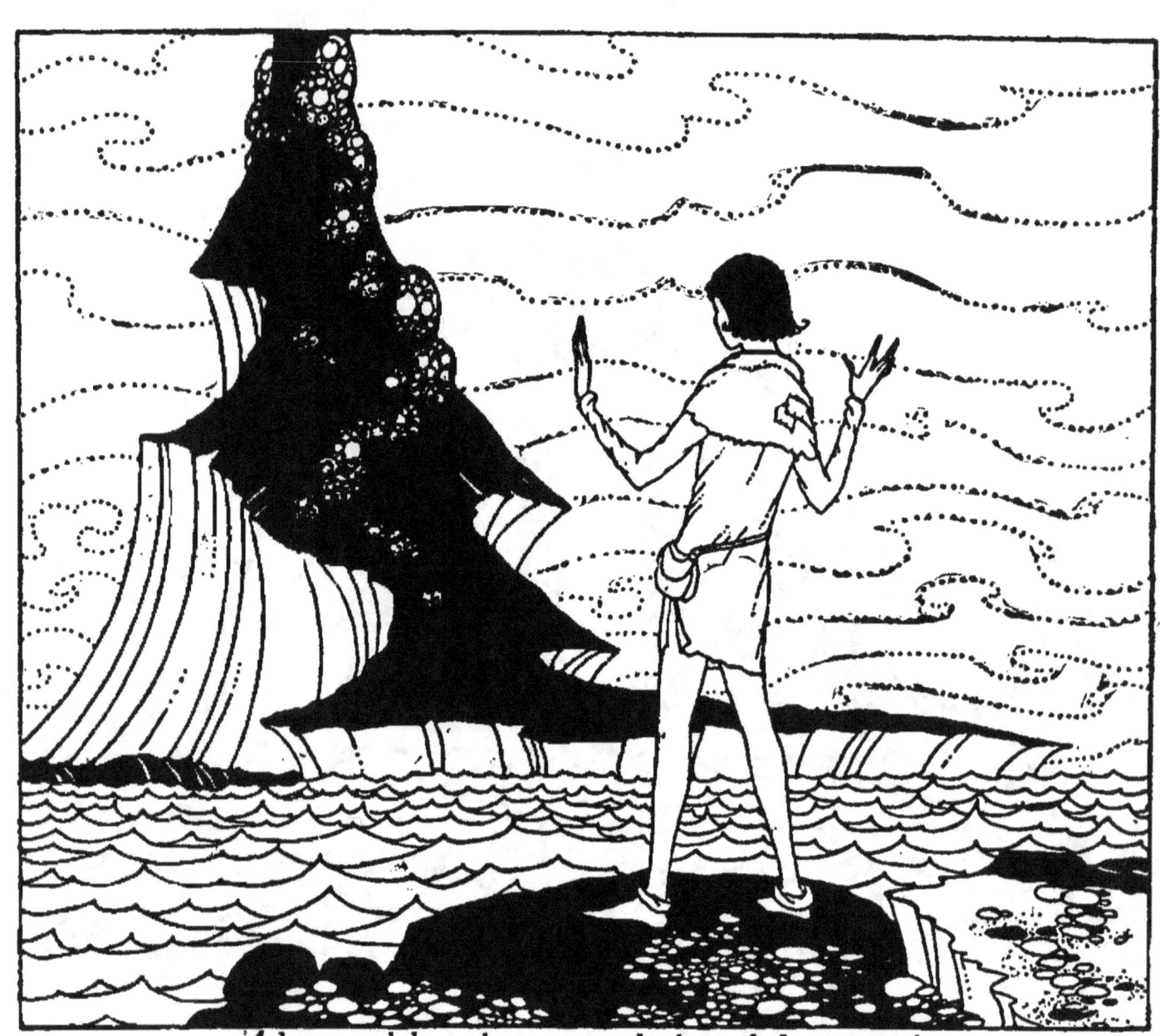
A large and deep river ran at the foot of the mountain

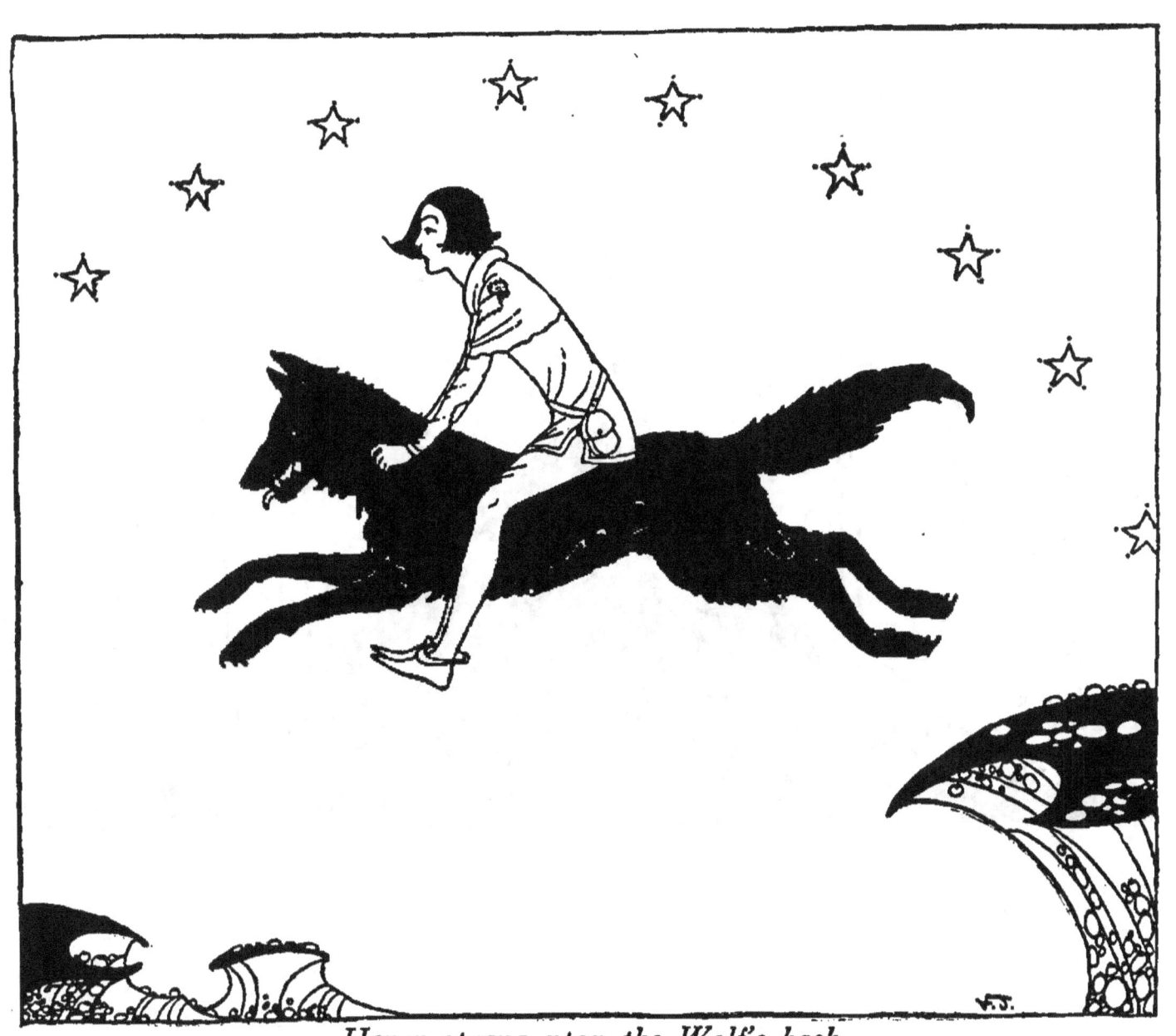
Henry sprang upon the Wolf's back

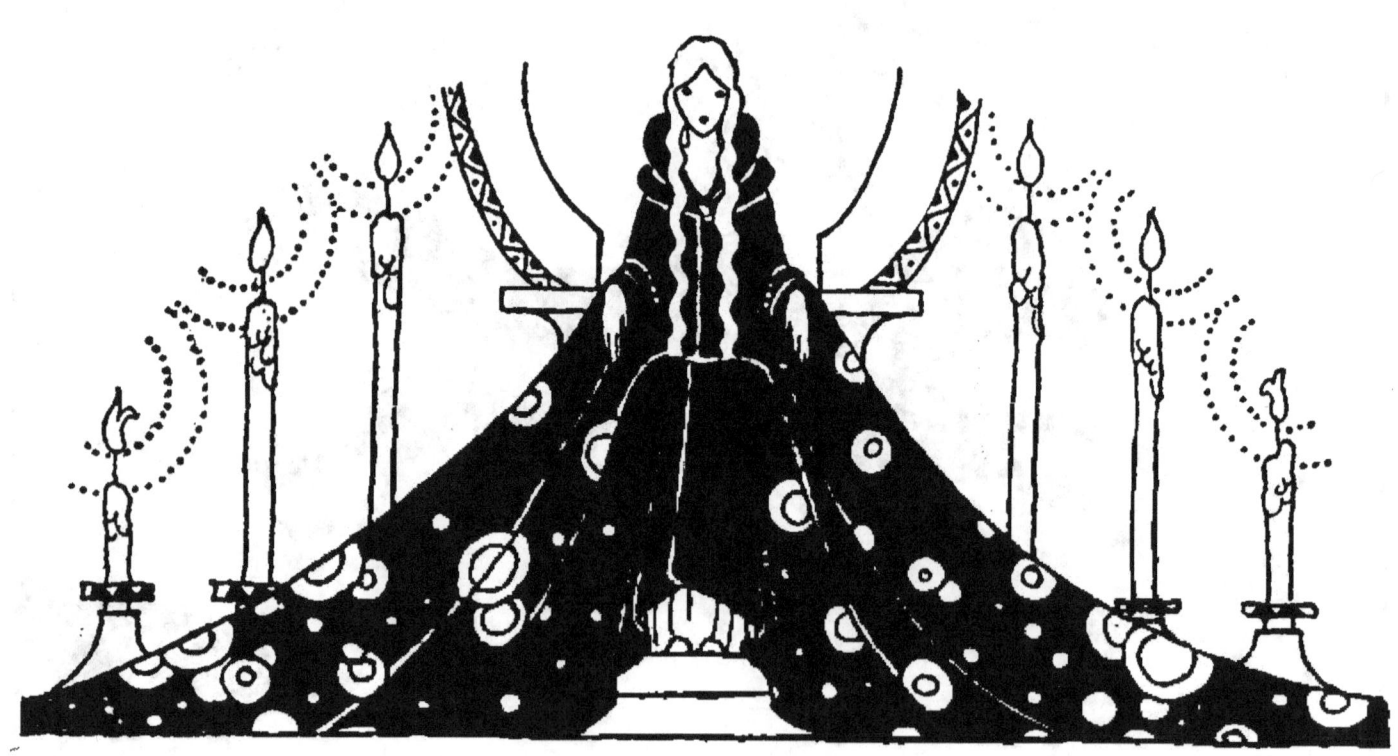

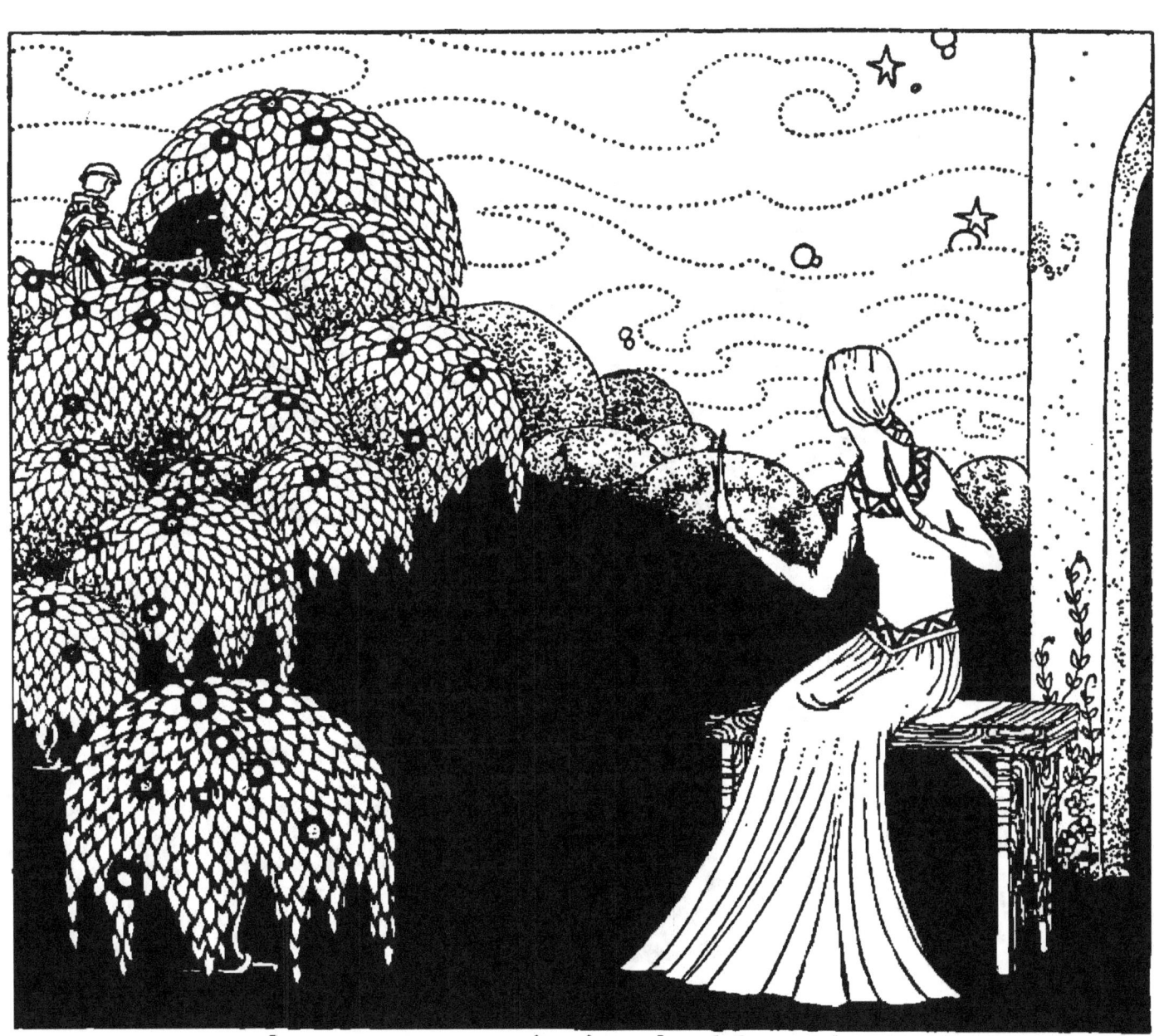

She saw a man arrive in a laced hat and coat

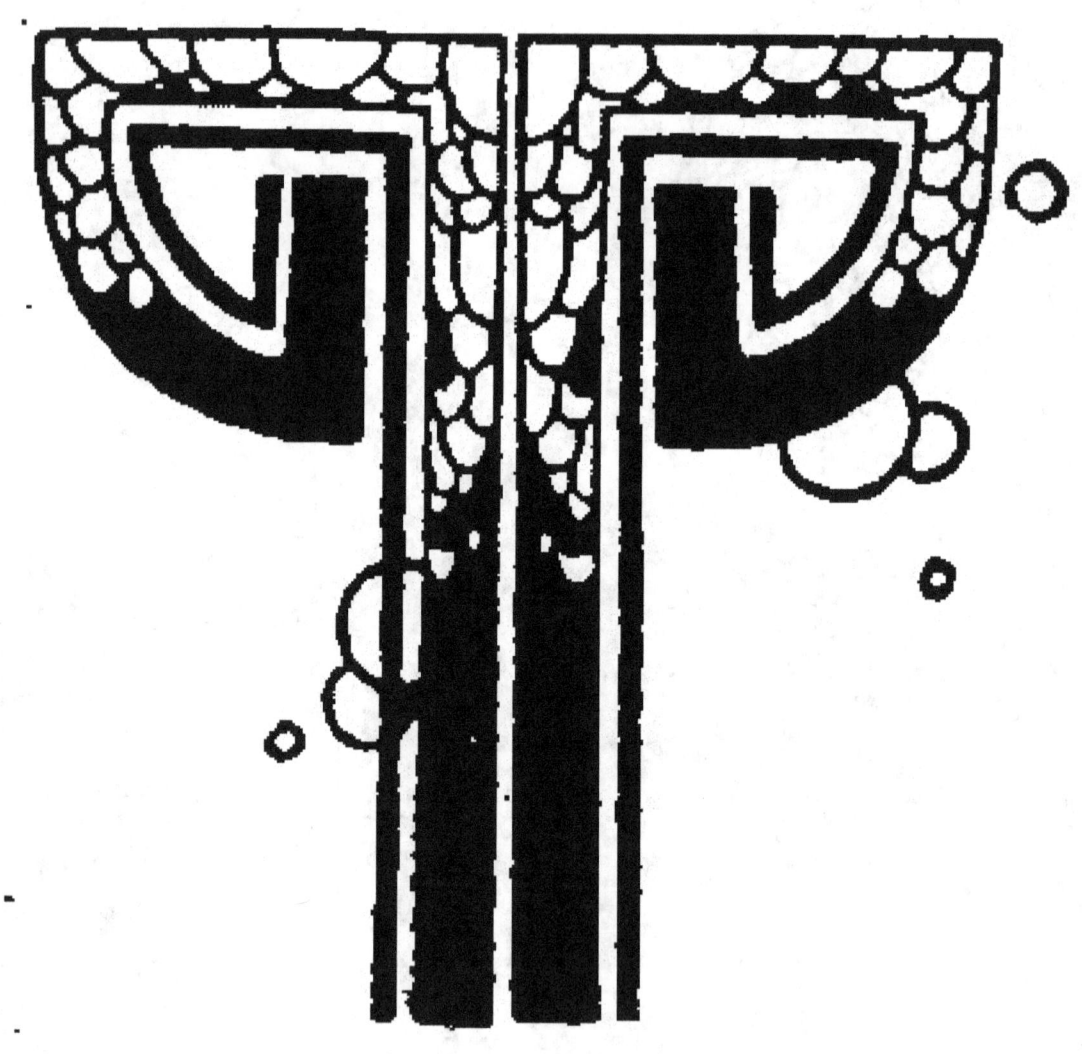

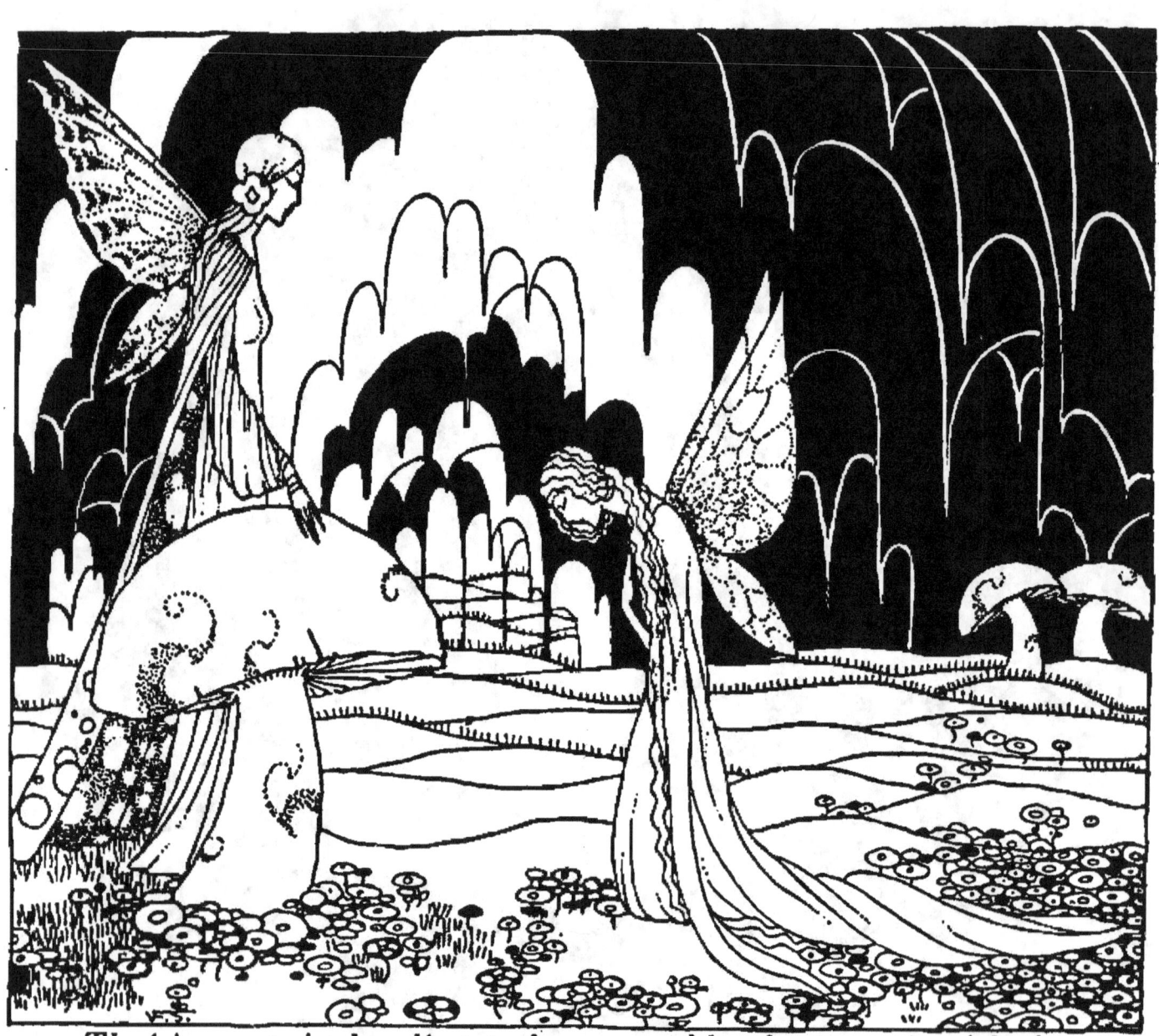
The fairy must give herself up to the queen and lose her power for eight days

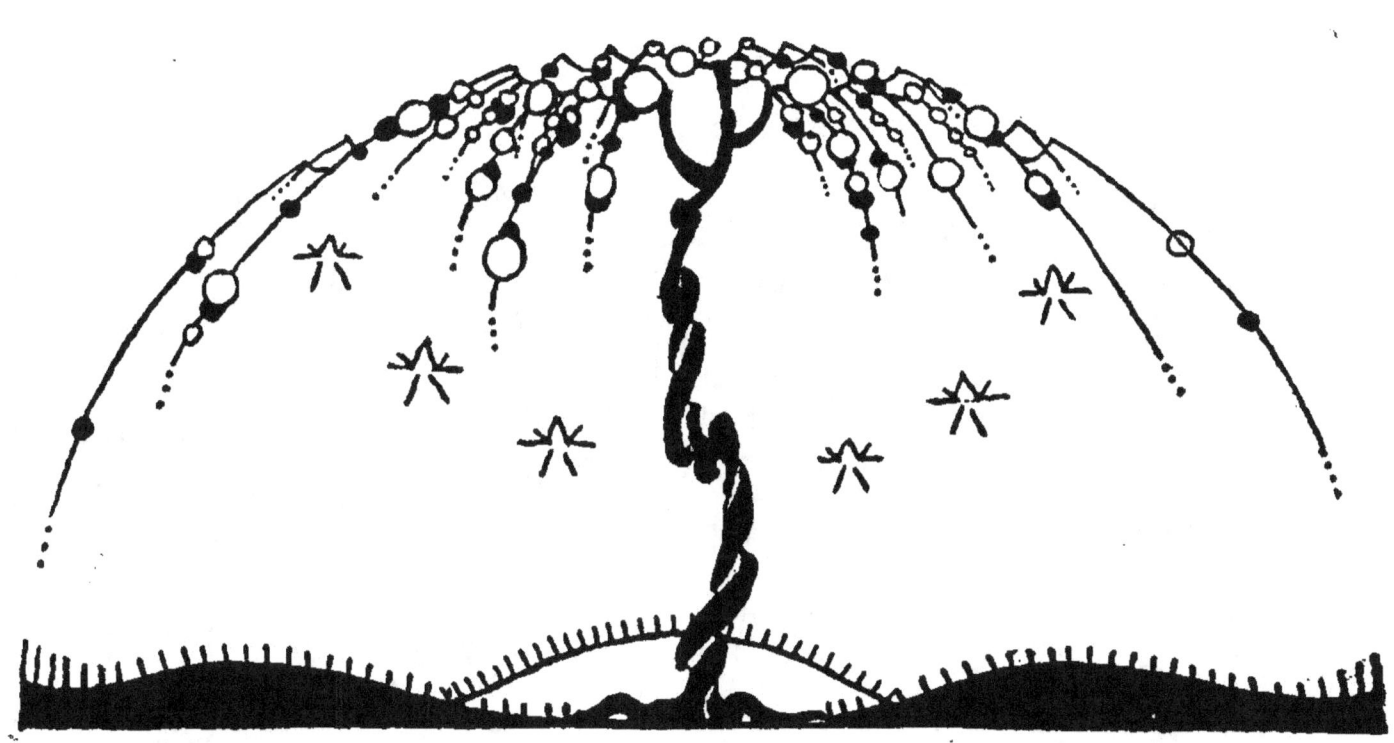

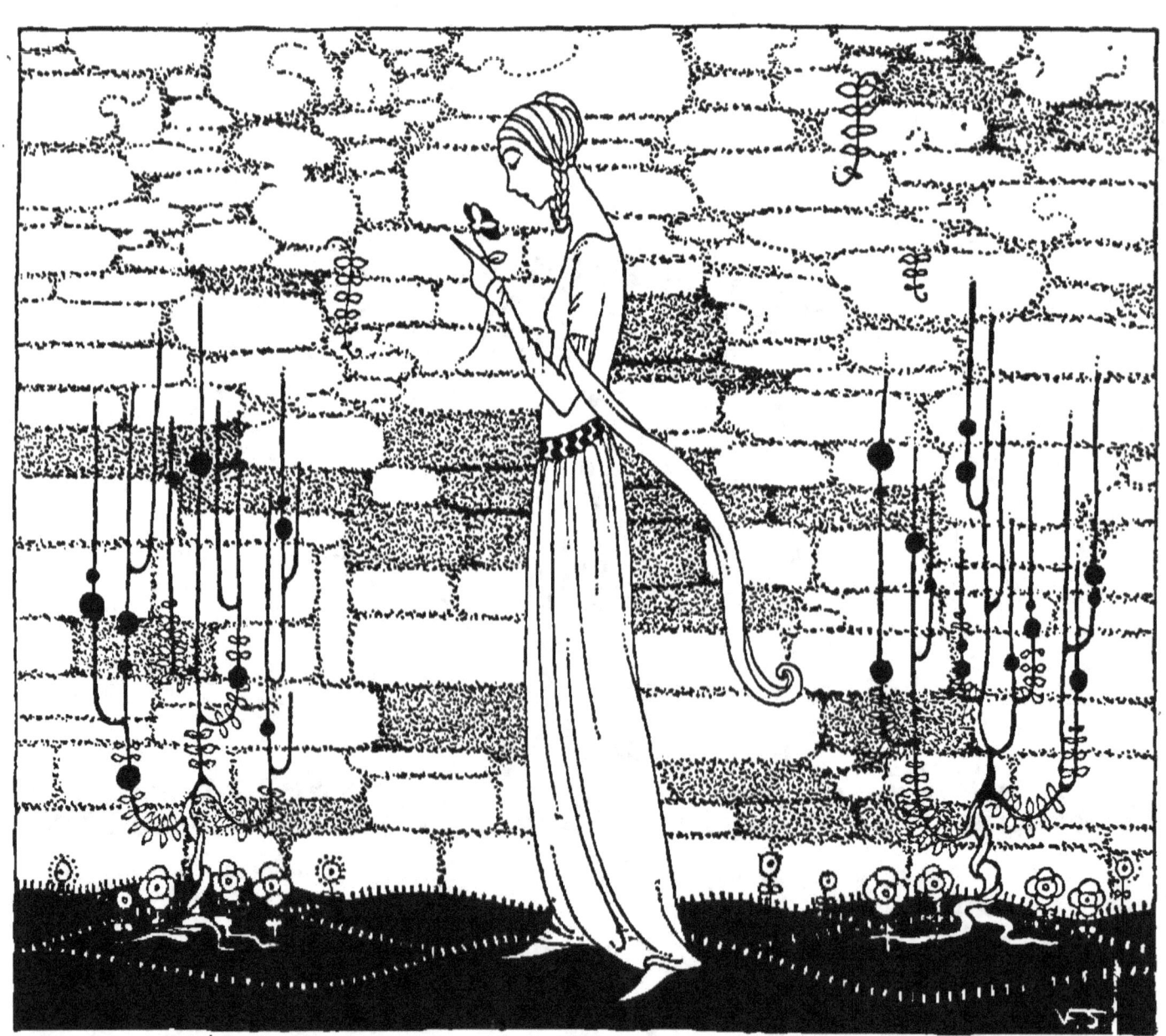

Rosalie never left the park, which was surrounded by high walls

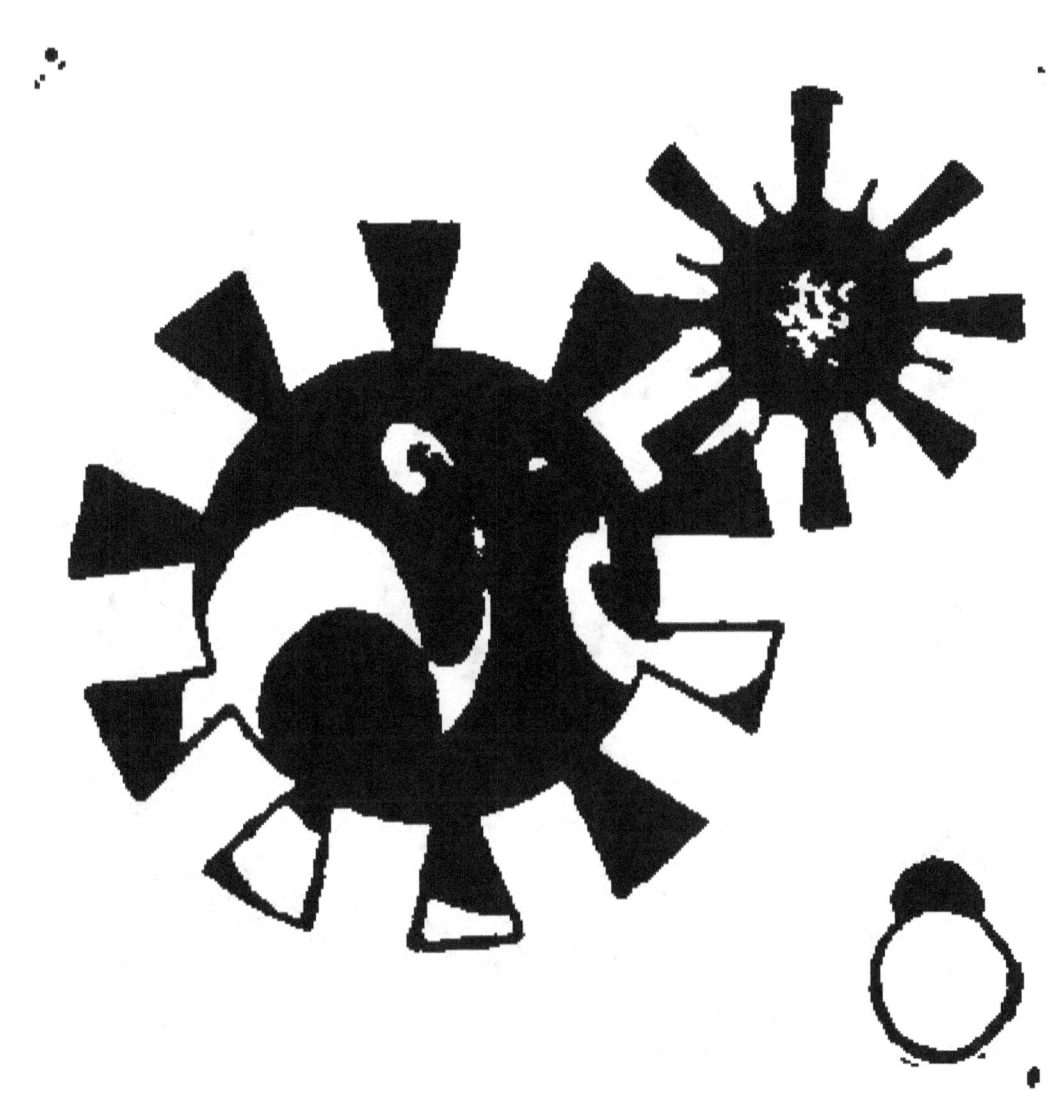

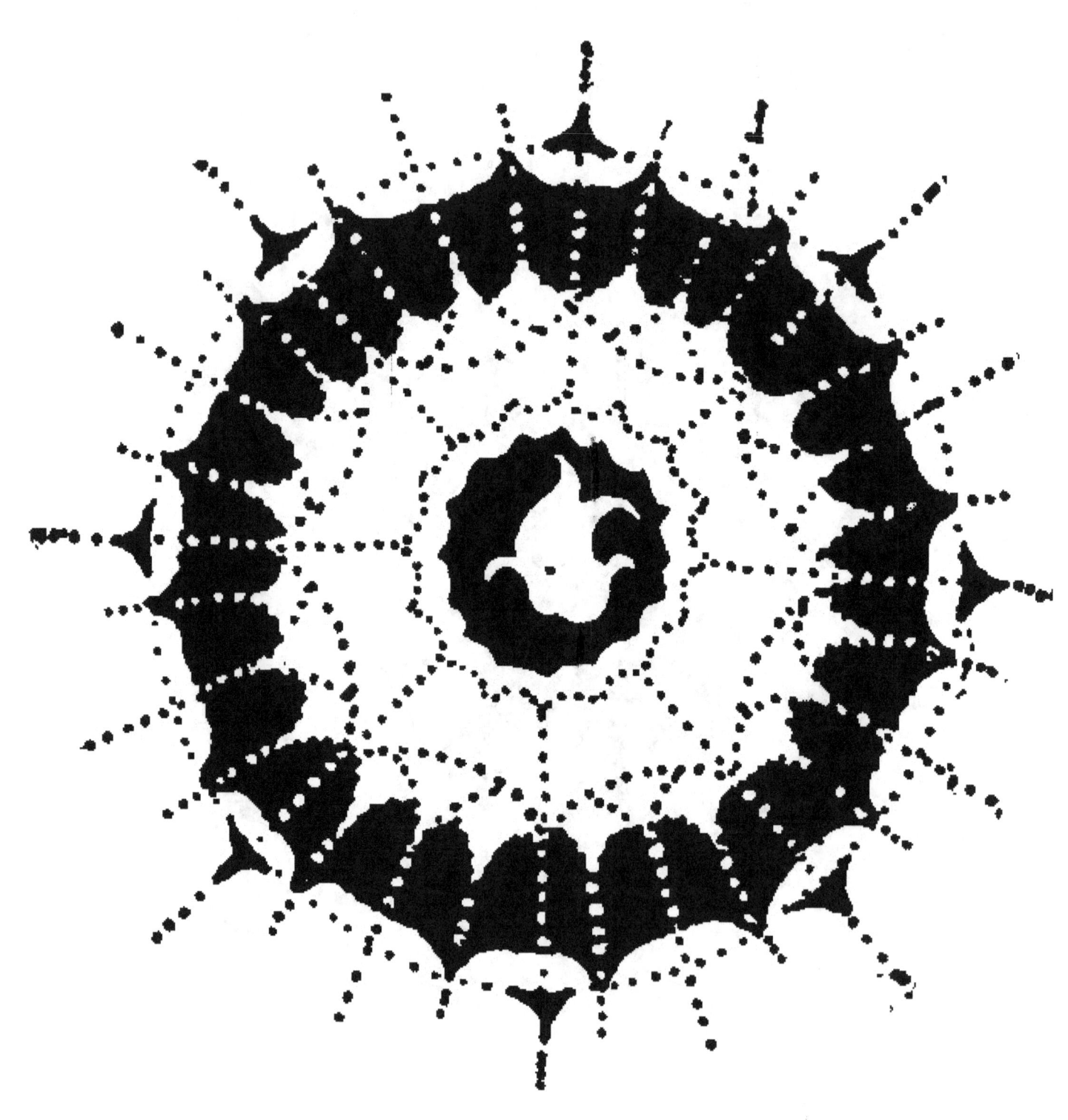

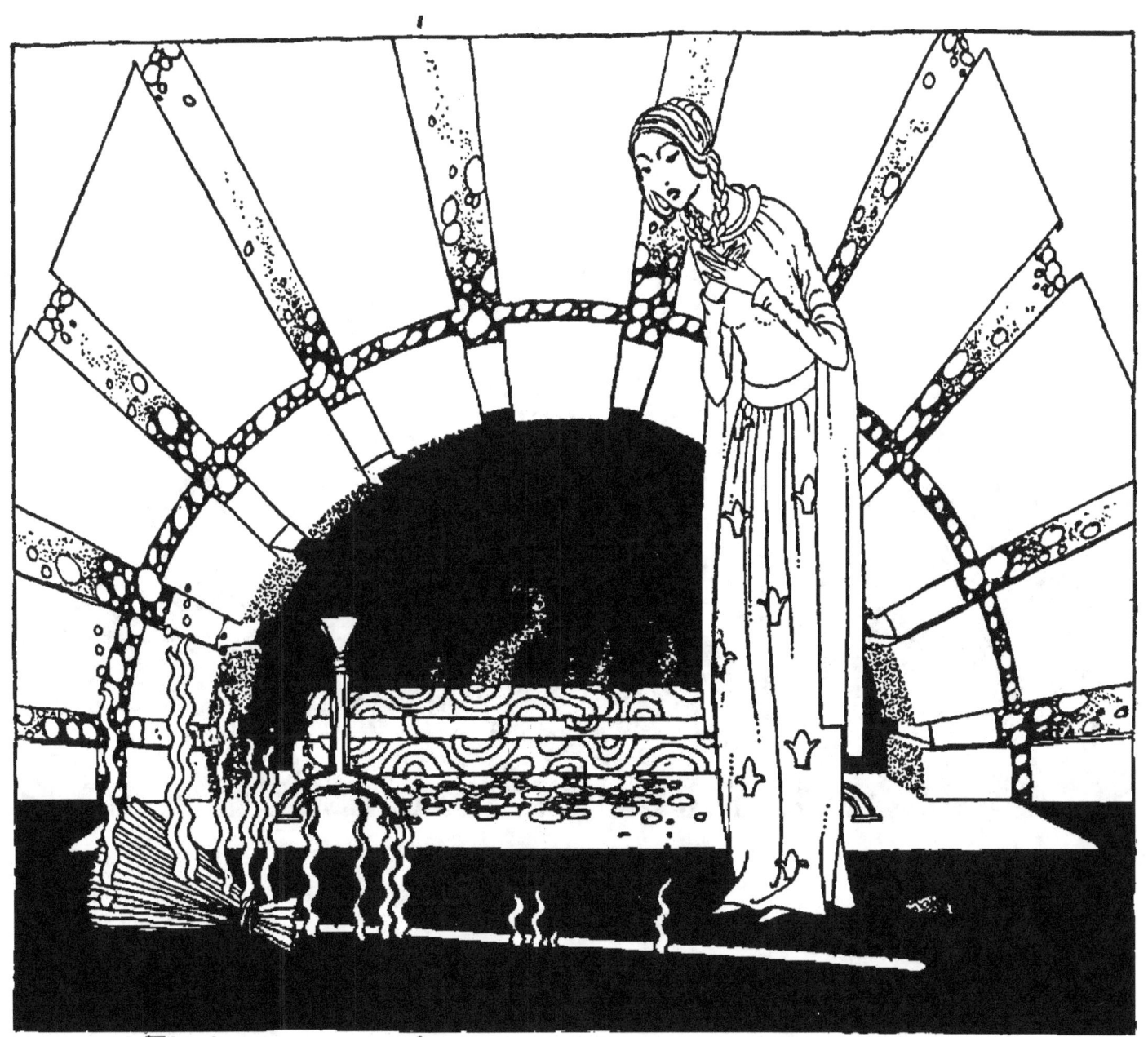

The broom was on fire at once, blazed up and burned her hands

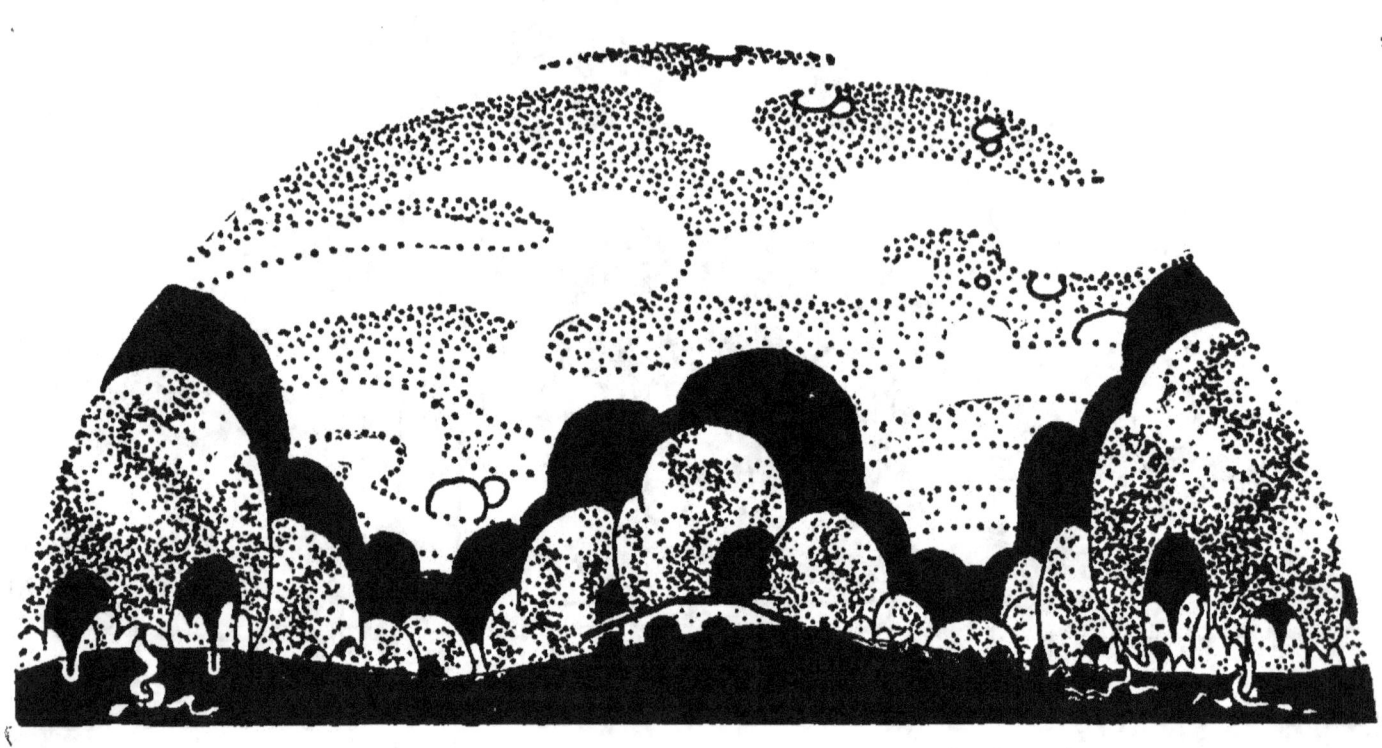

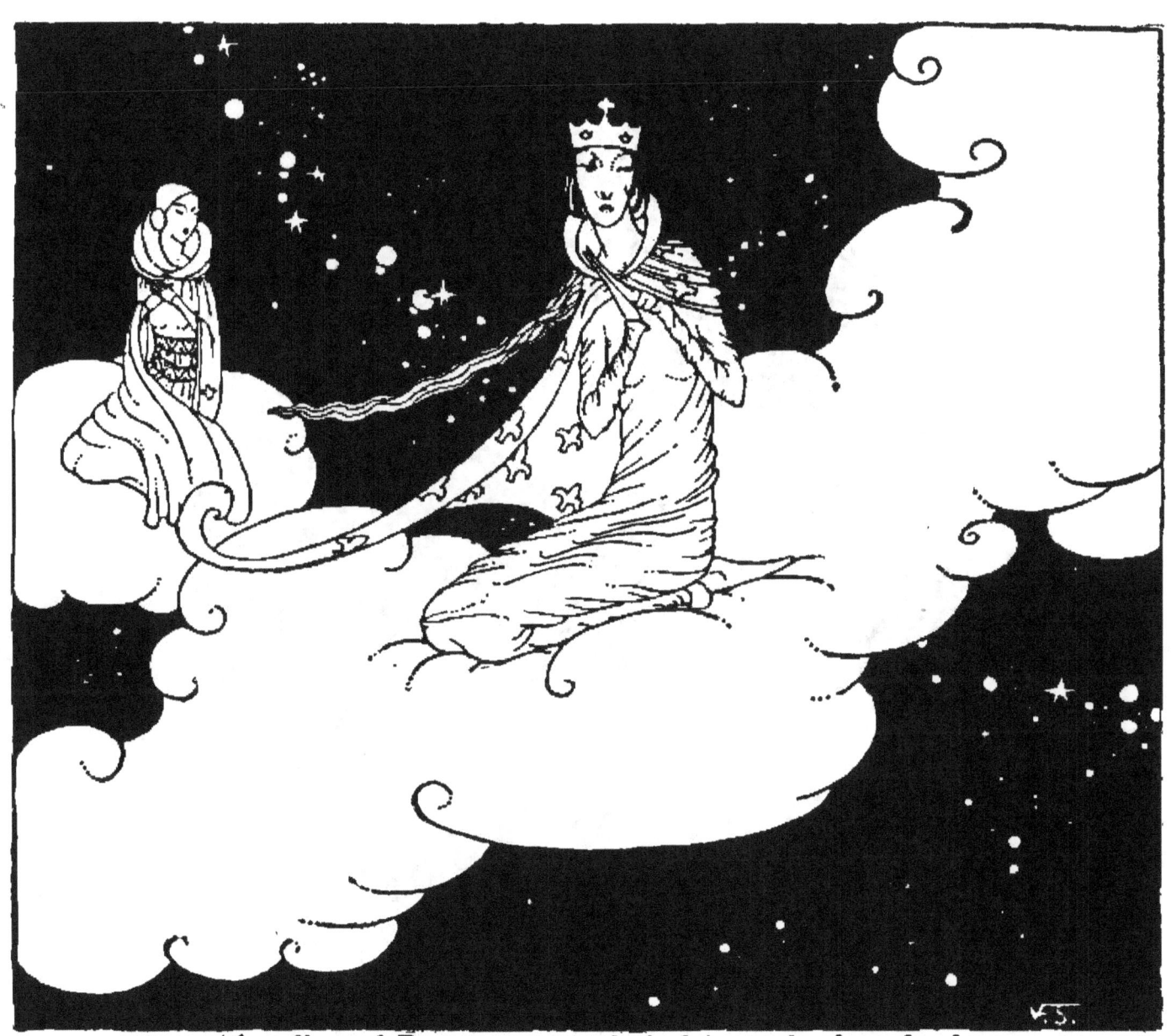
Agnella and Passerose were dashed from cloud to cloud

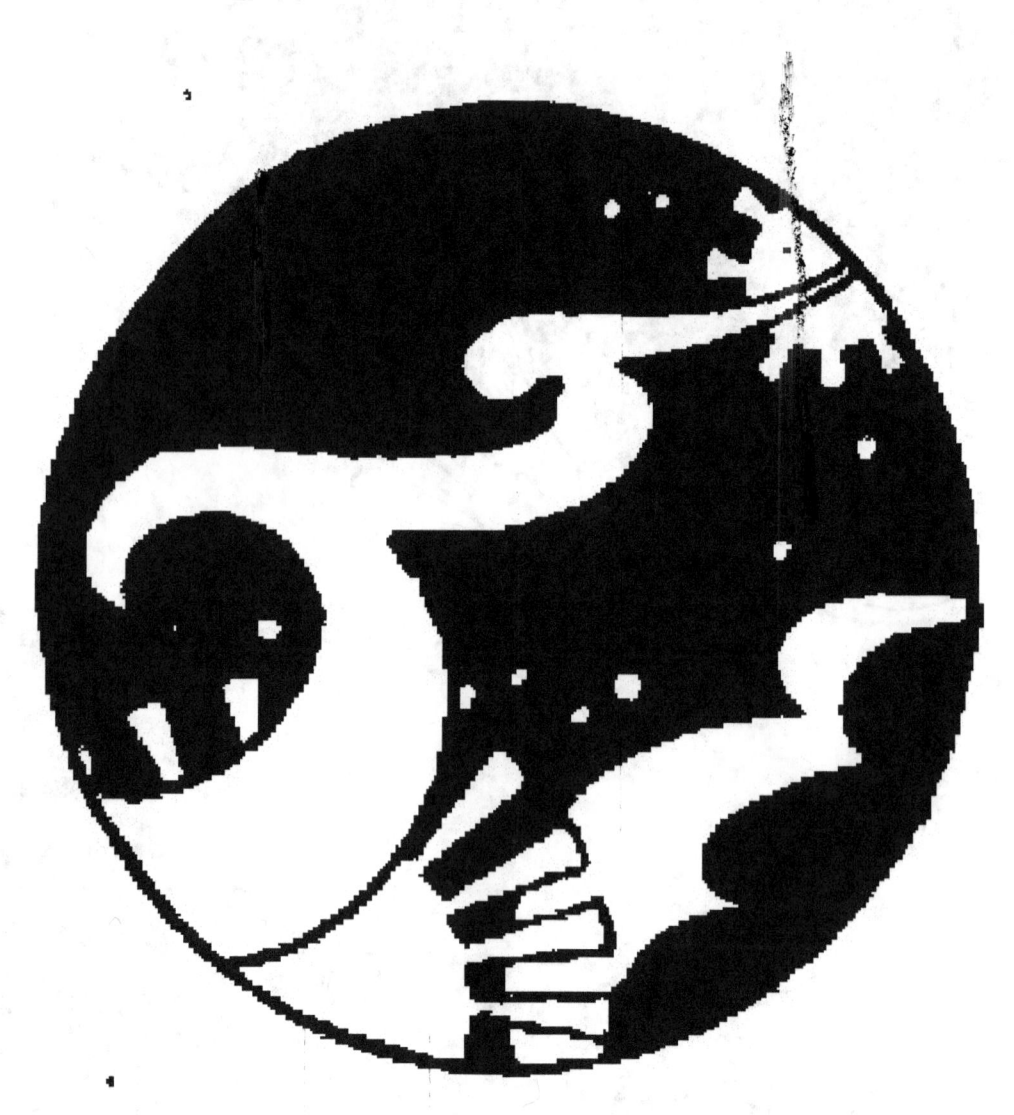

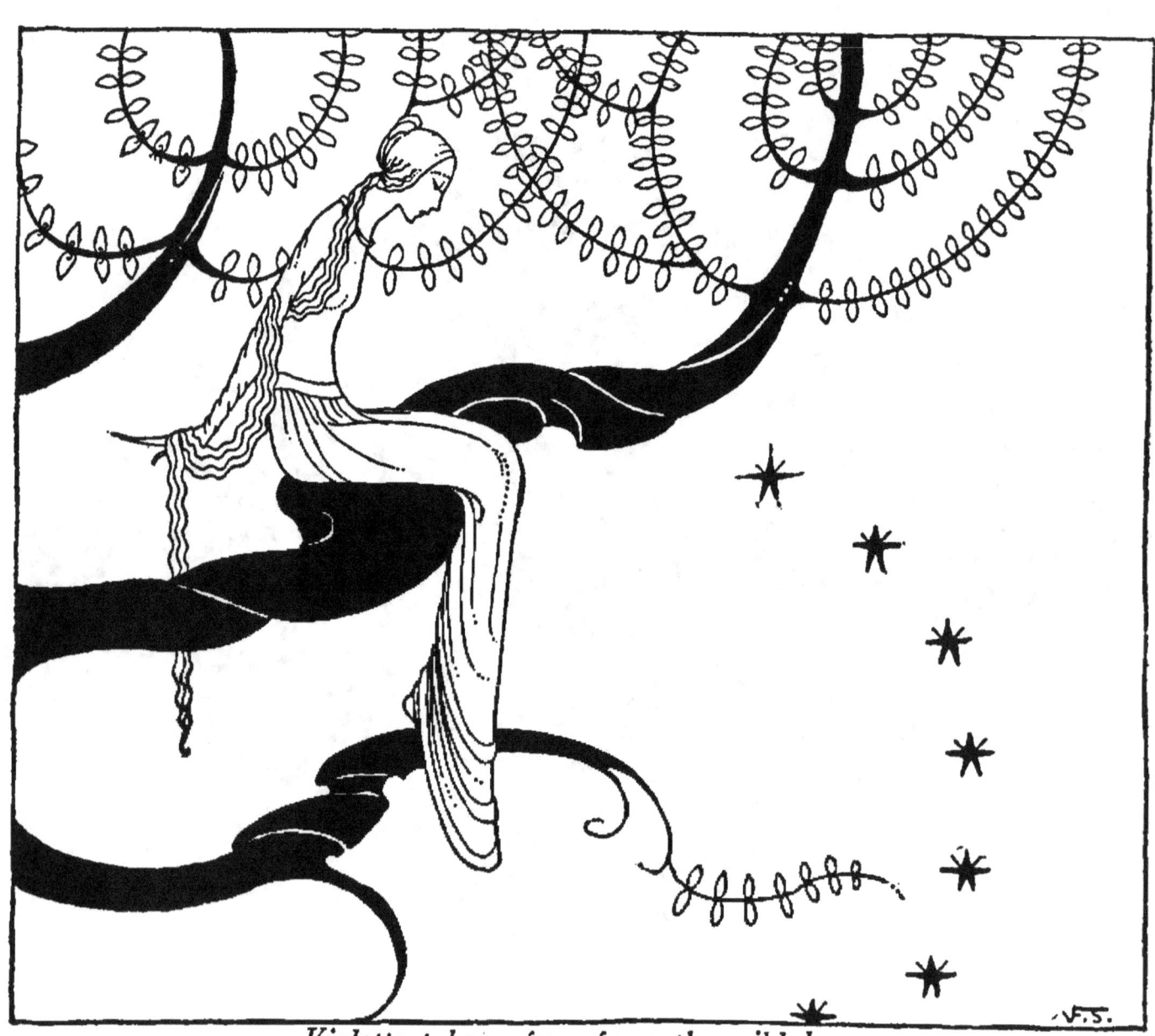
Violette takes refuge from the wild boar

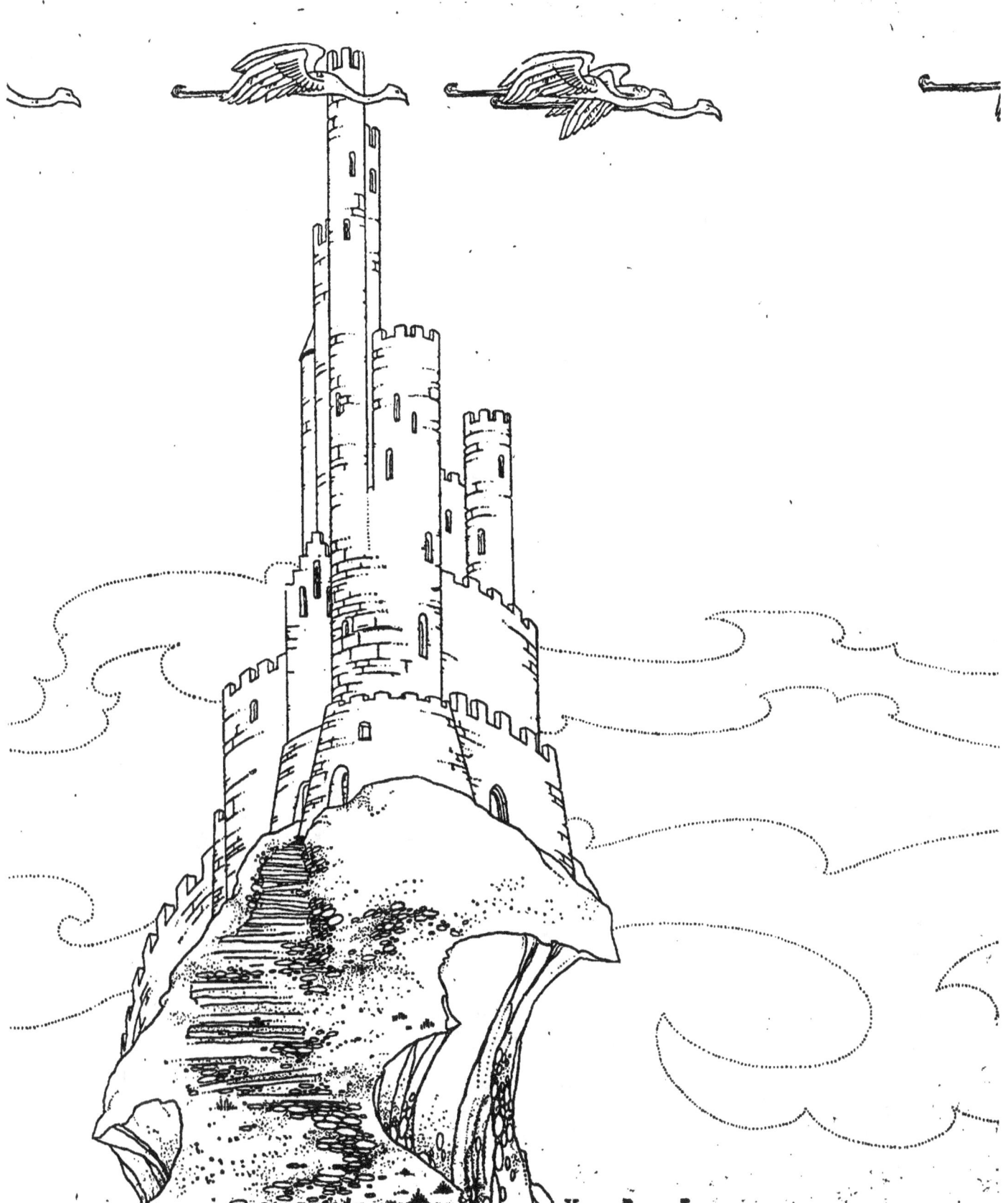

Tanglewood Tales

Illustrated by
Virginia Frances Sterrett

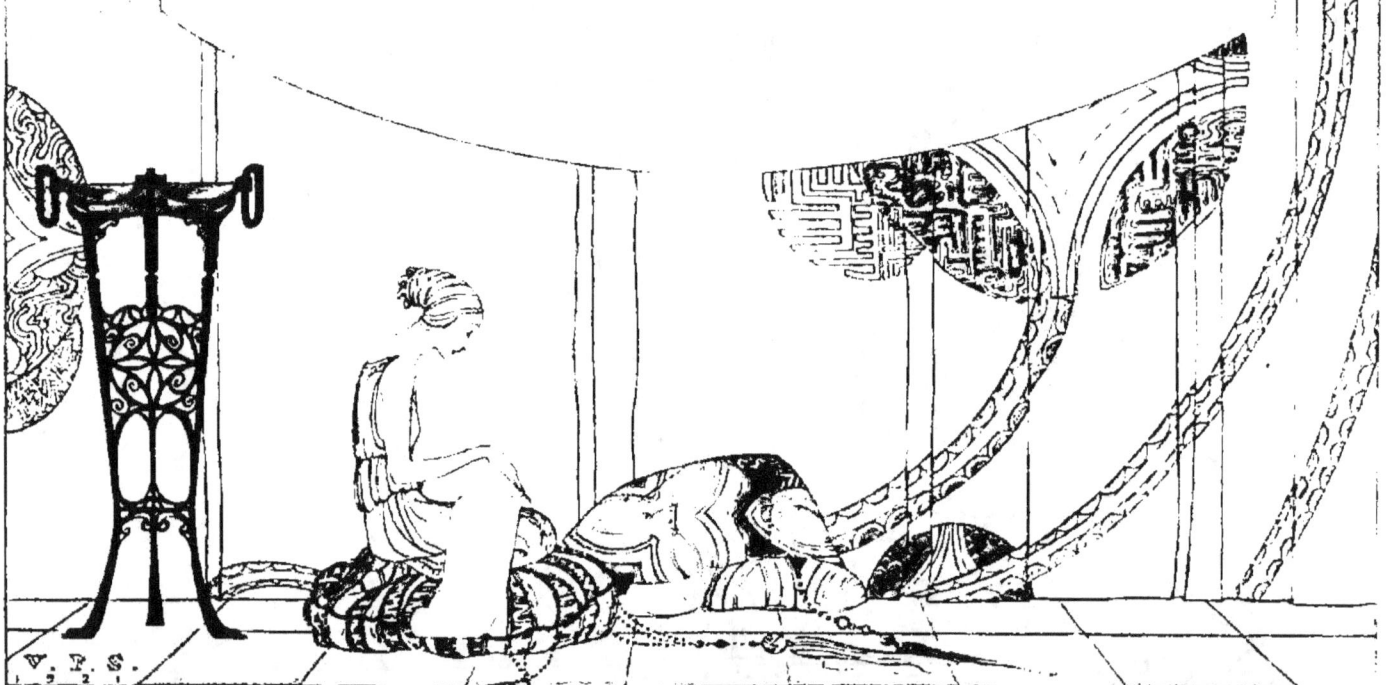

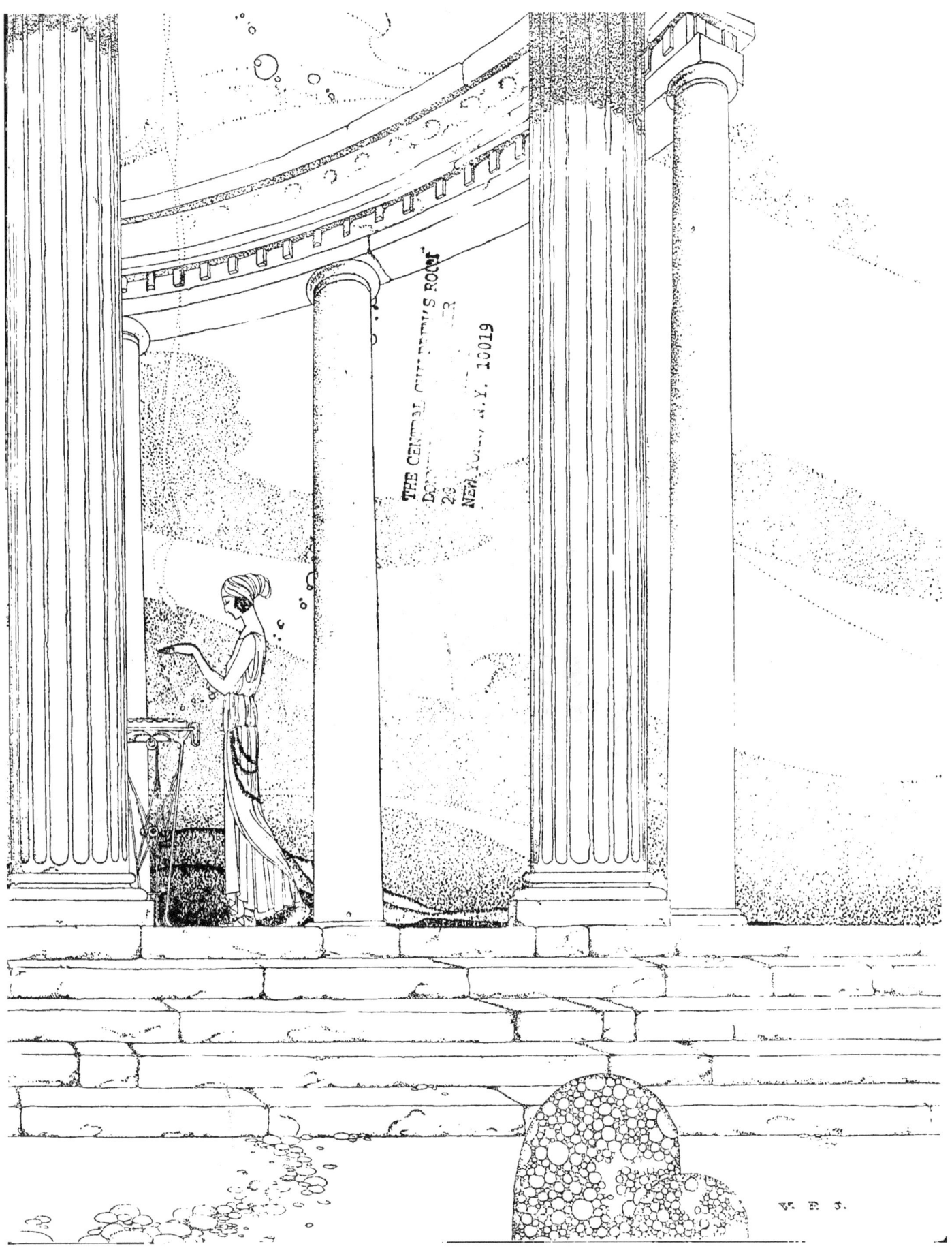

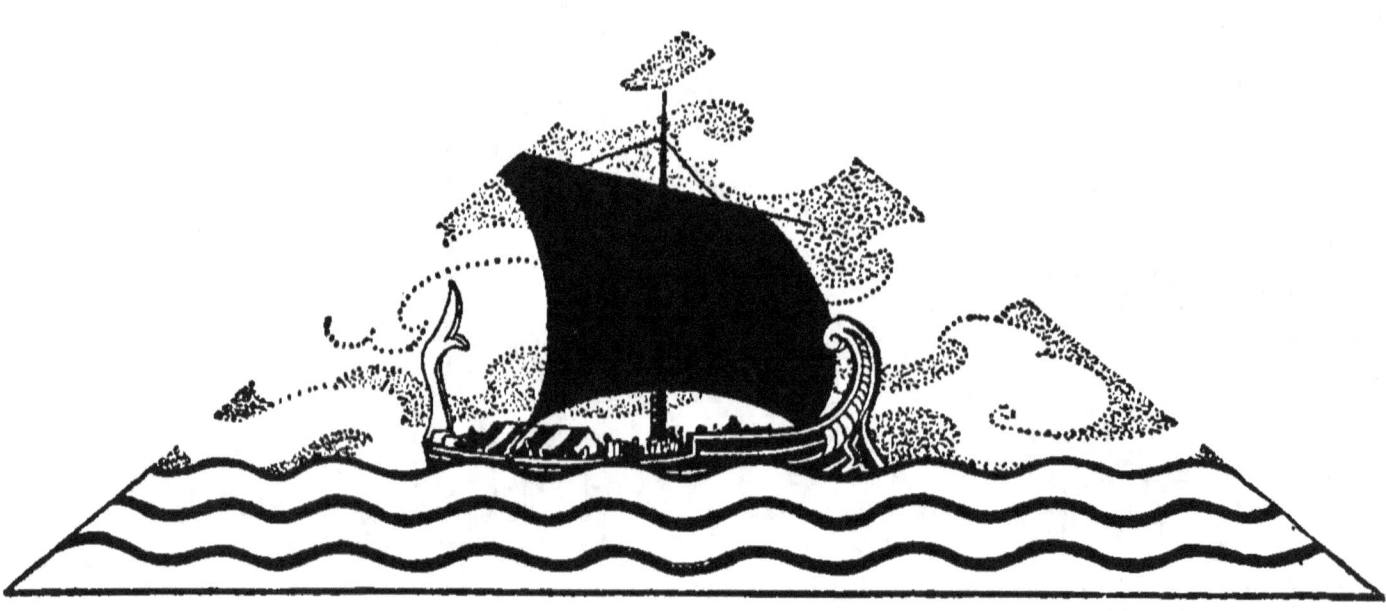

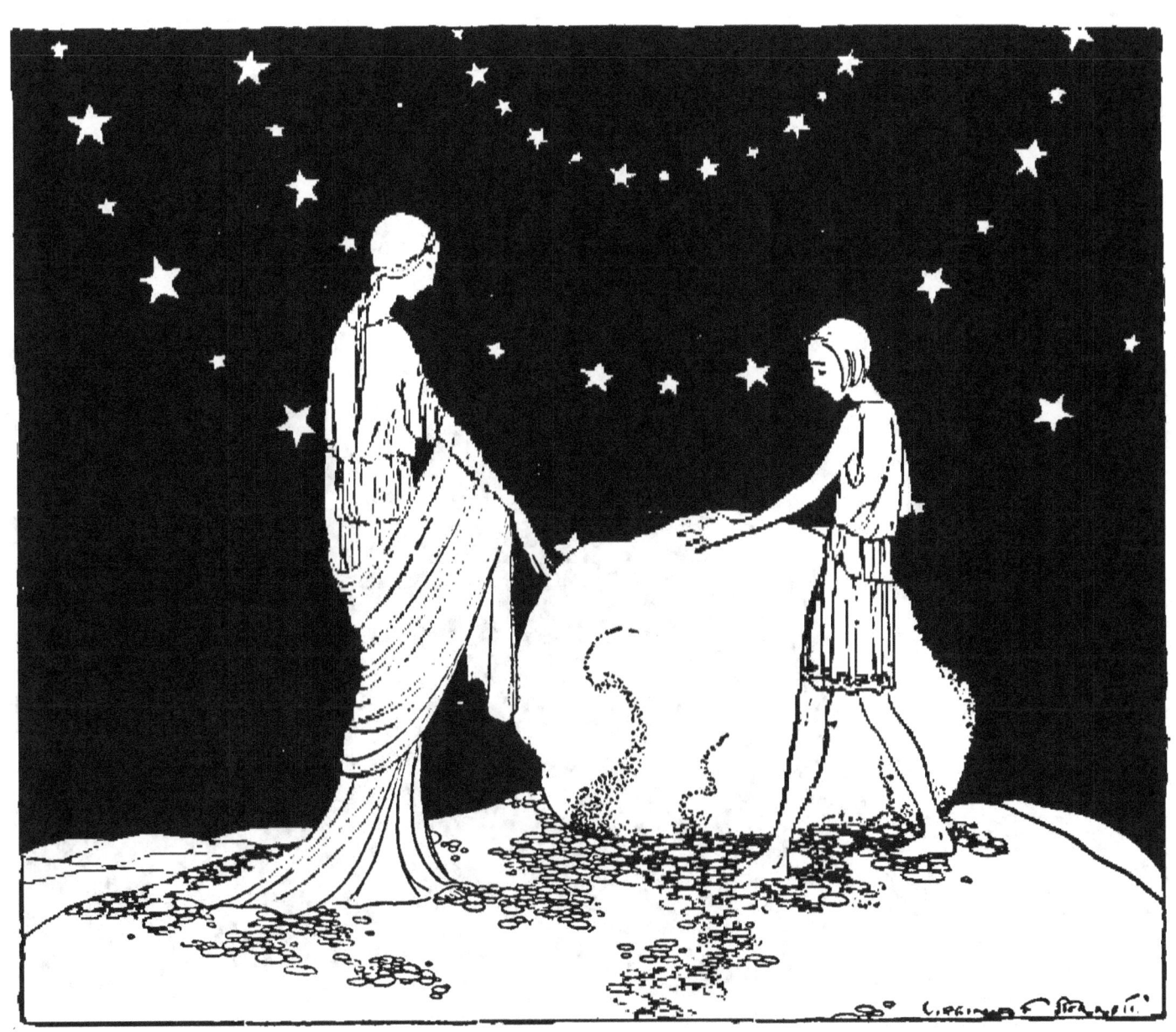

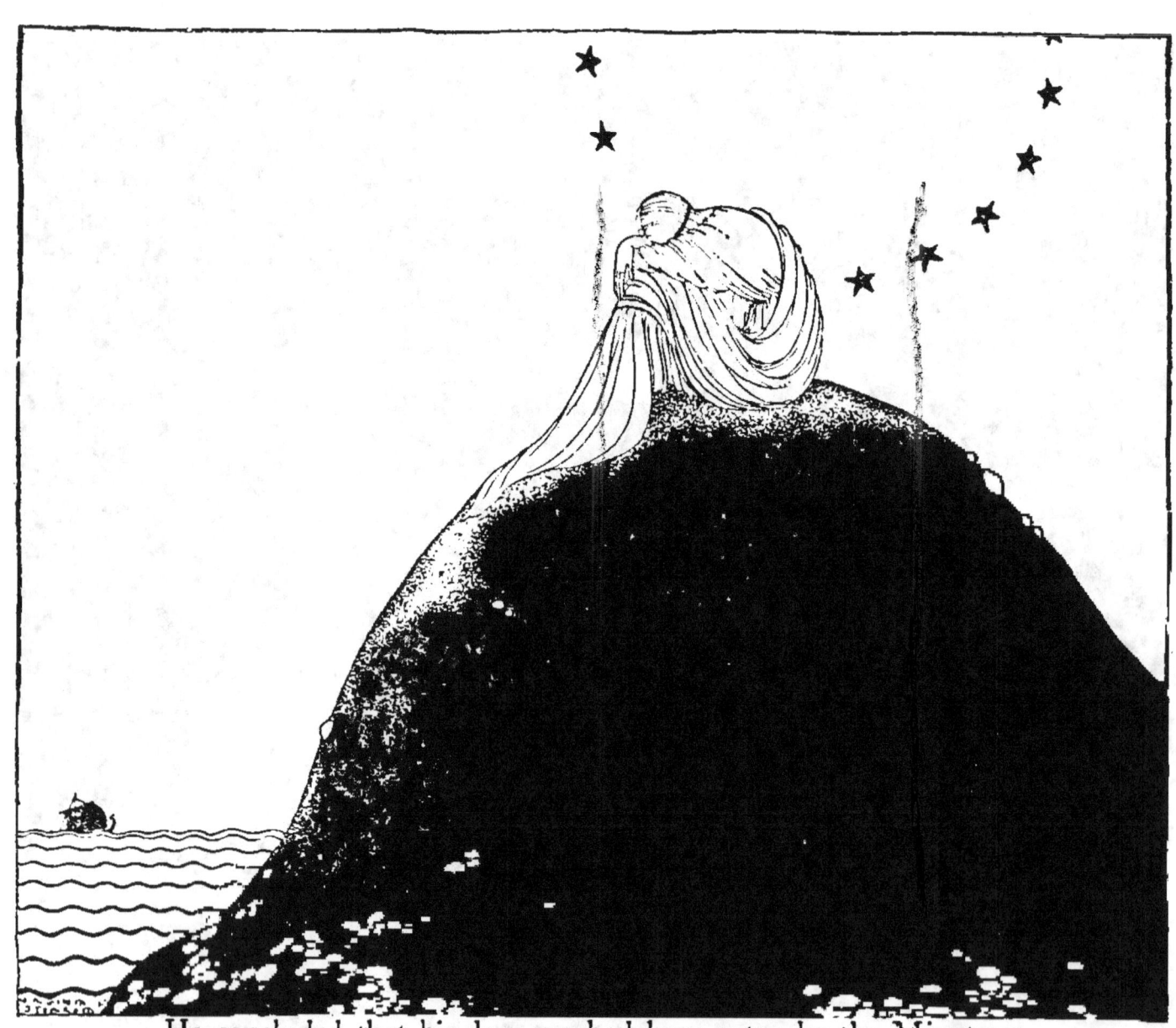
He concluded that his dear son had been eaten by the Minotaur.

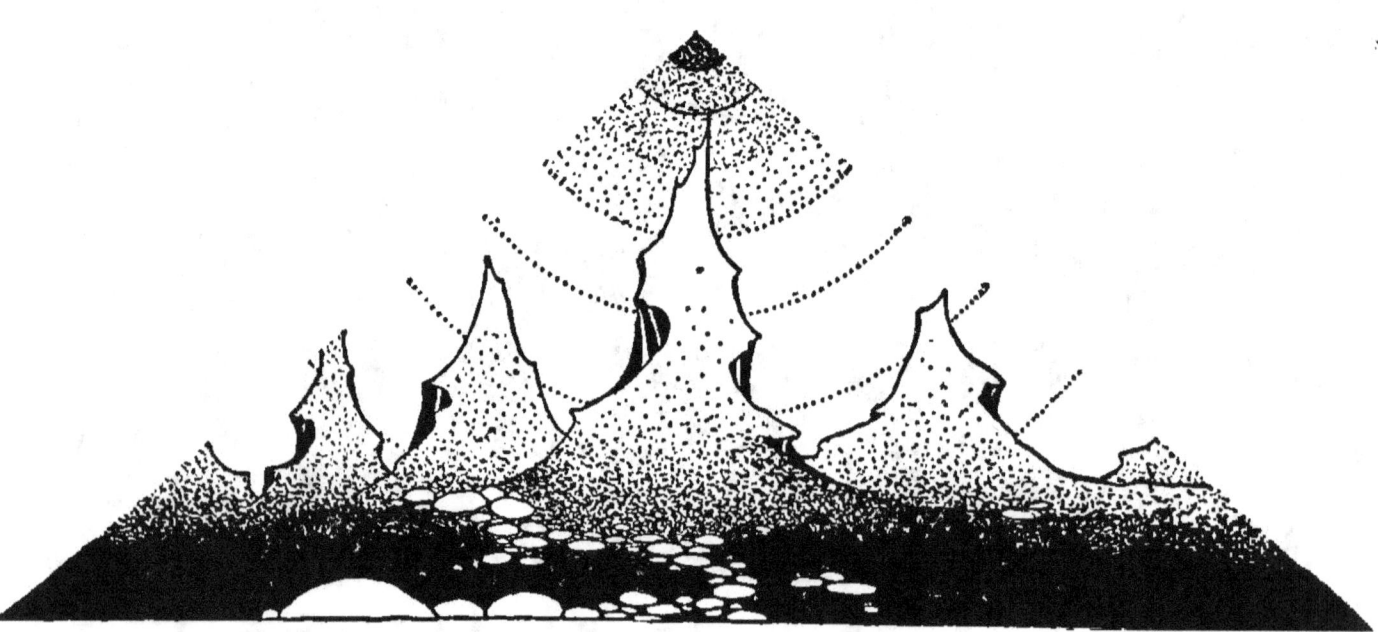

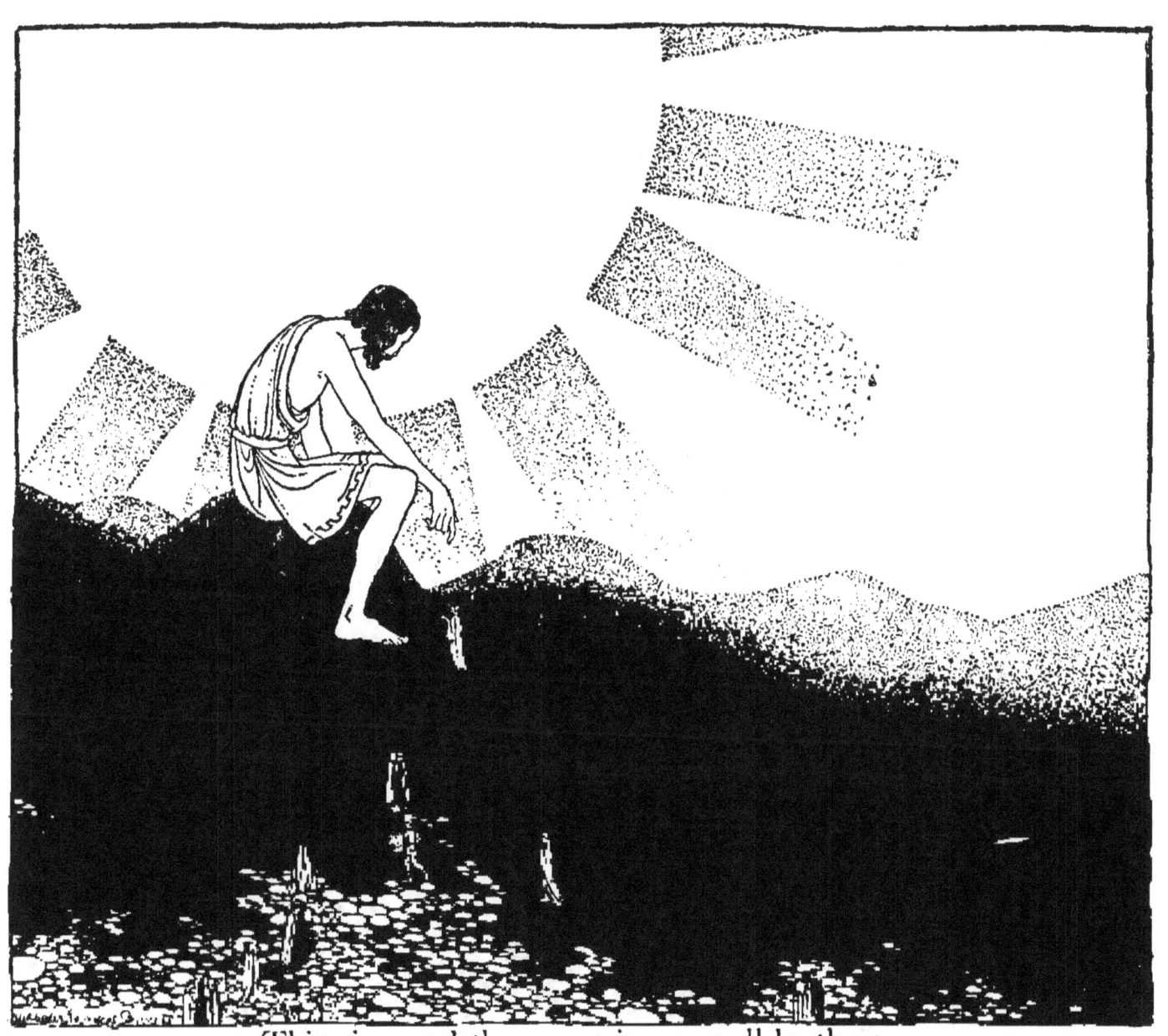
This giant and these pygmies were all brethren.

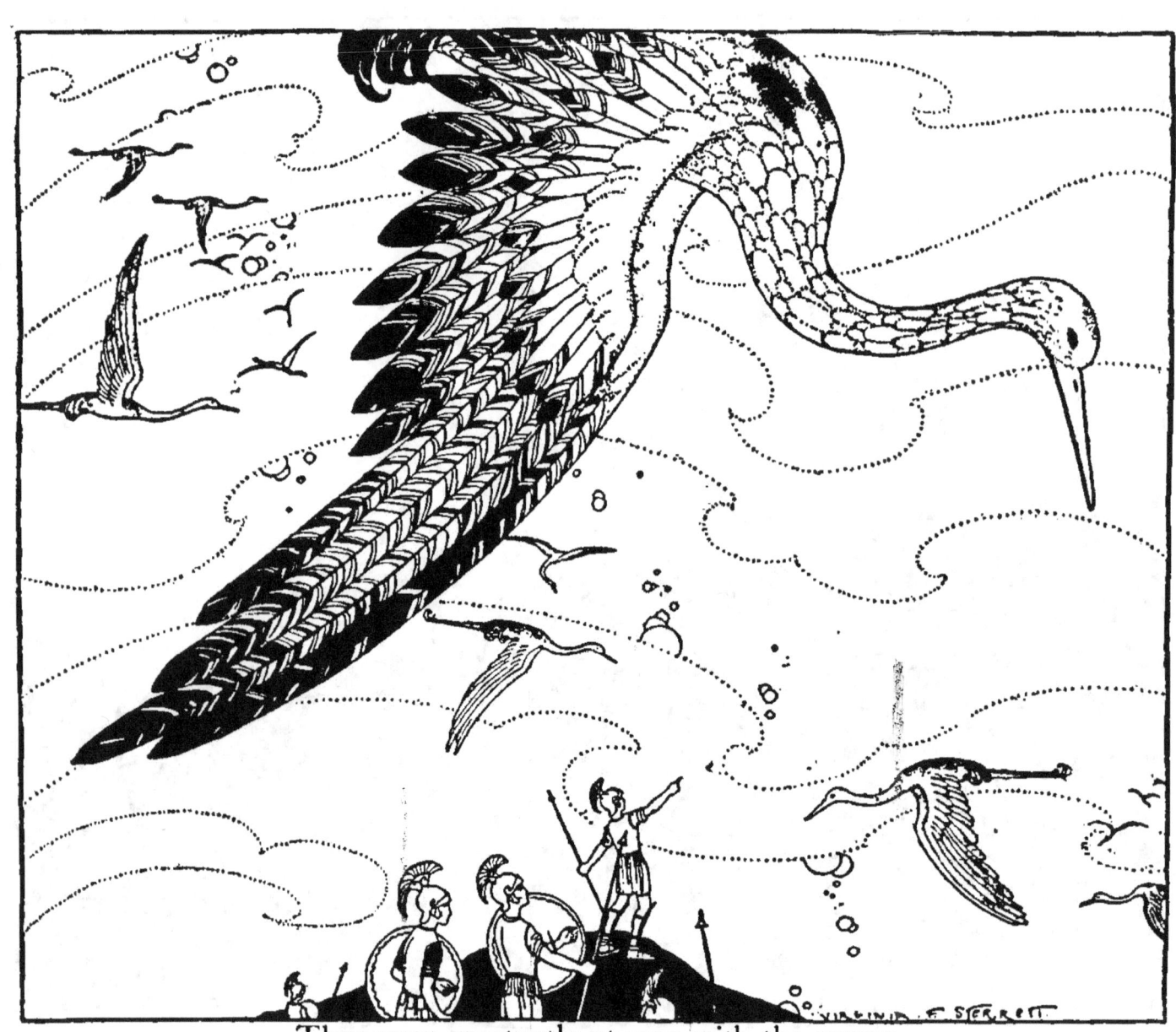
They were constantly at war with the cranes.

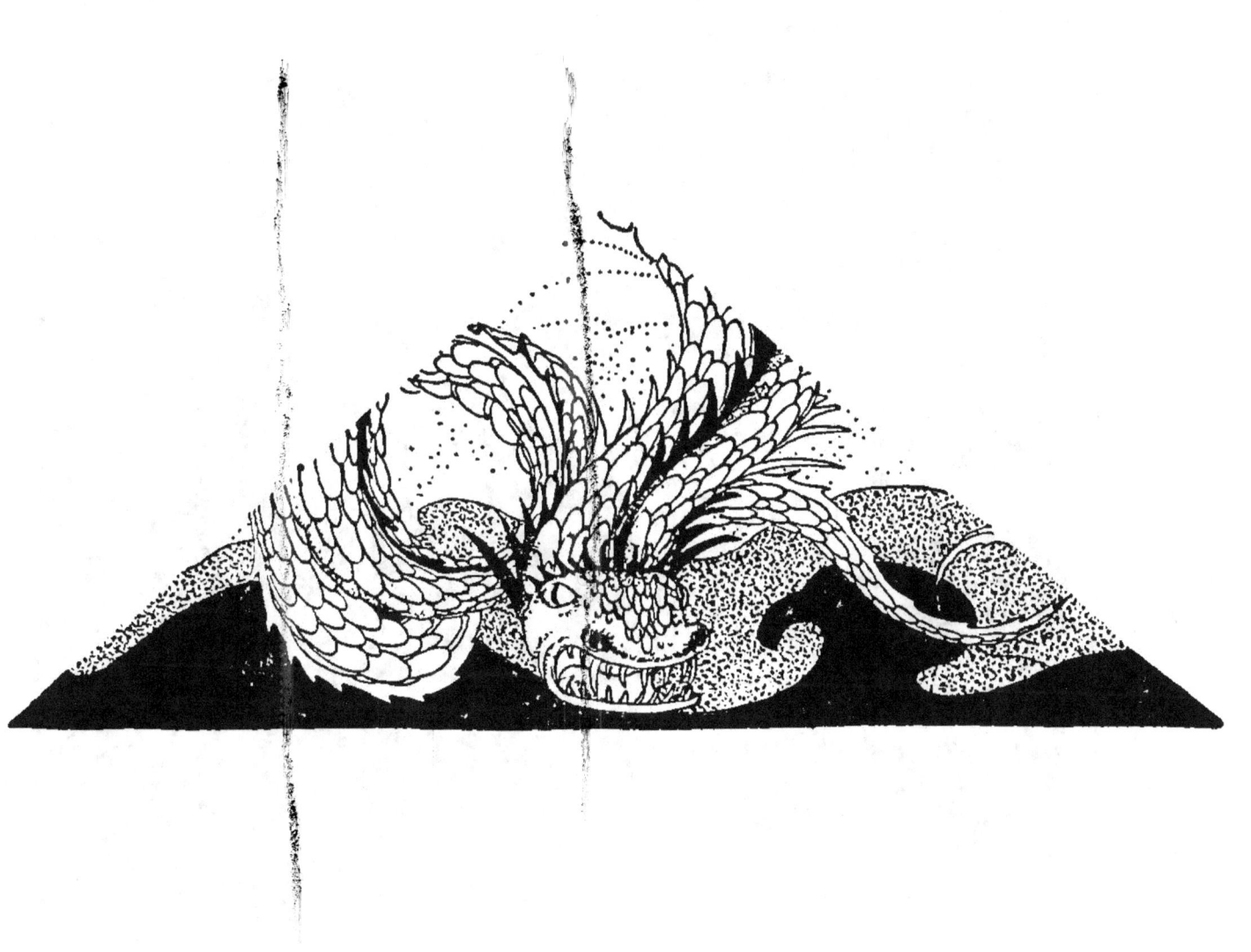

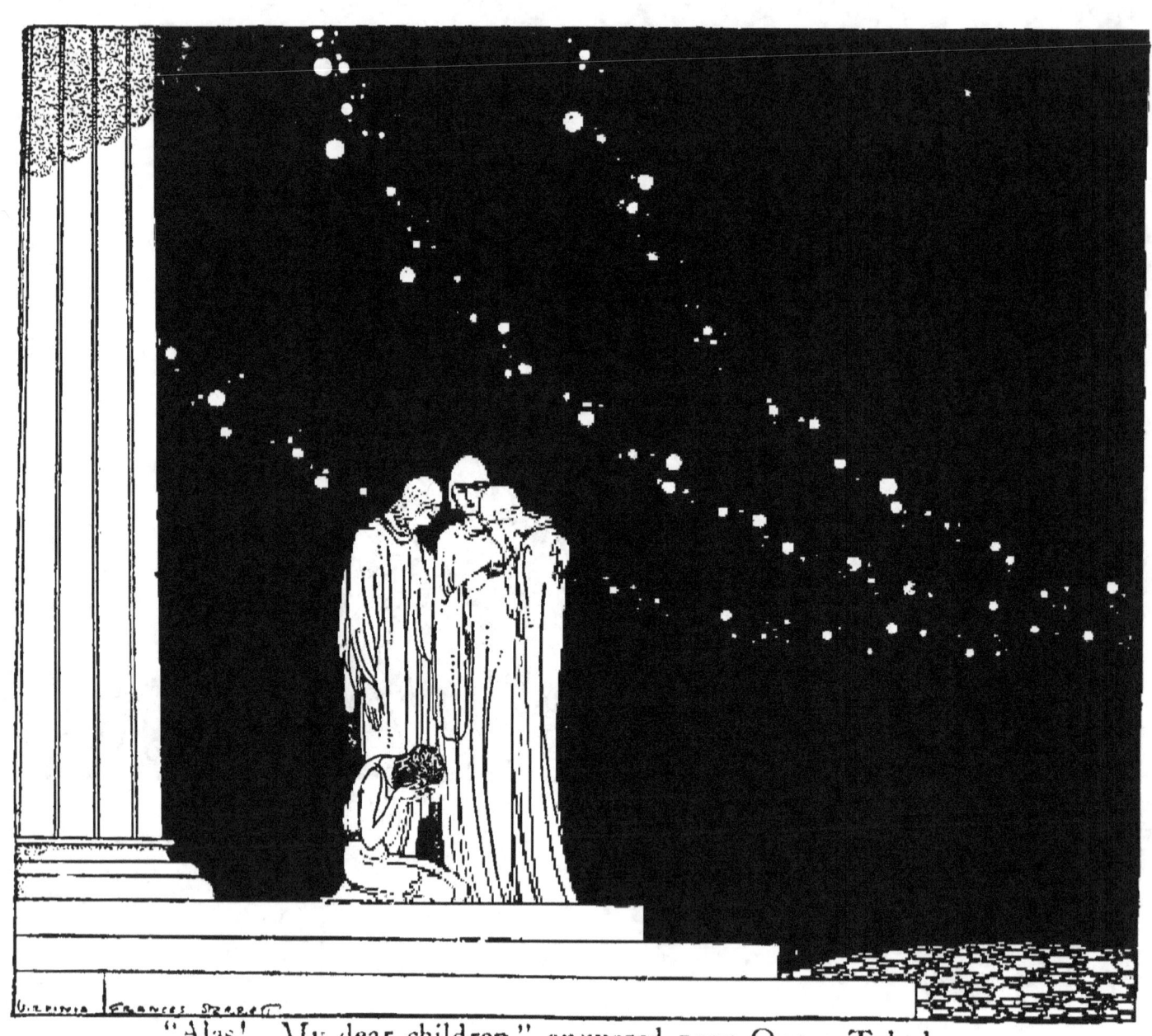
"Alas! My dear children," answered poor Queen Telephassa.

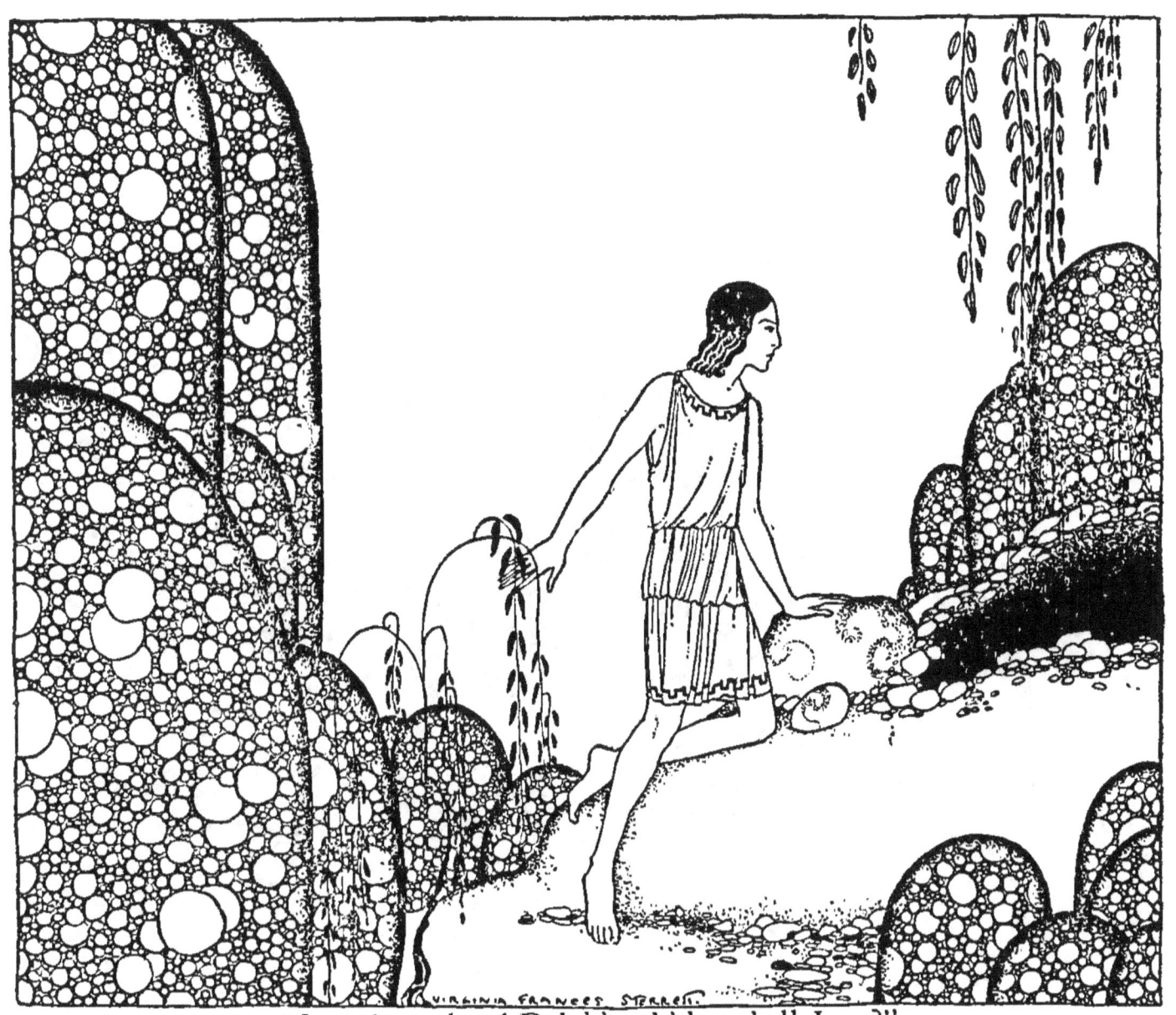
"Sacred oracle of Delphi, whither shall I go?"

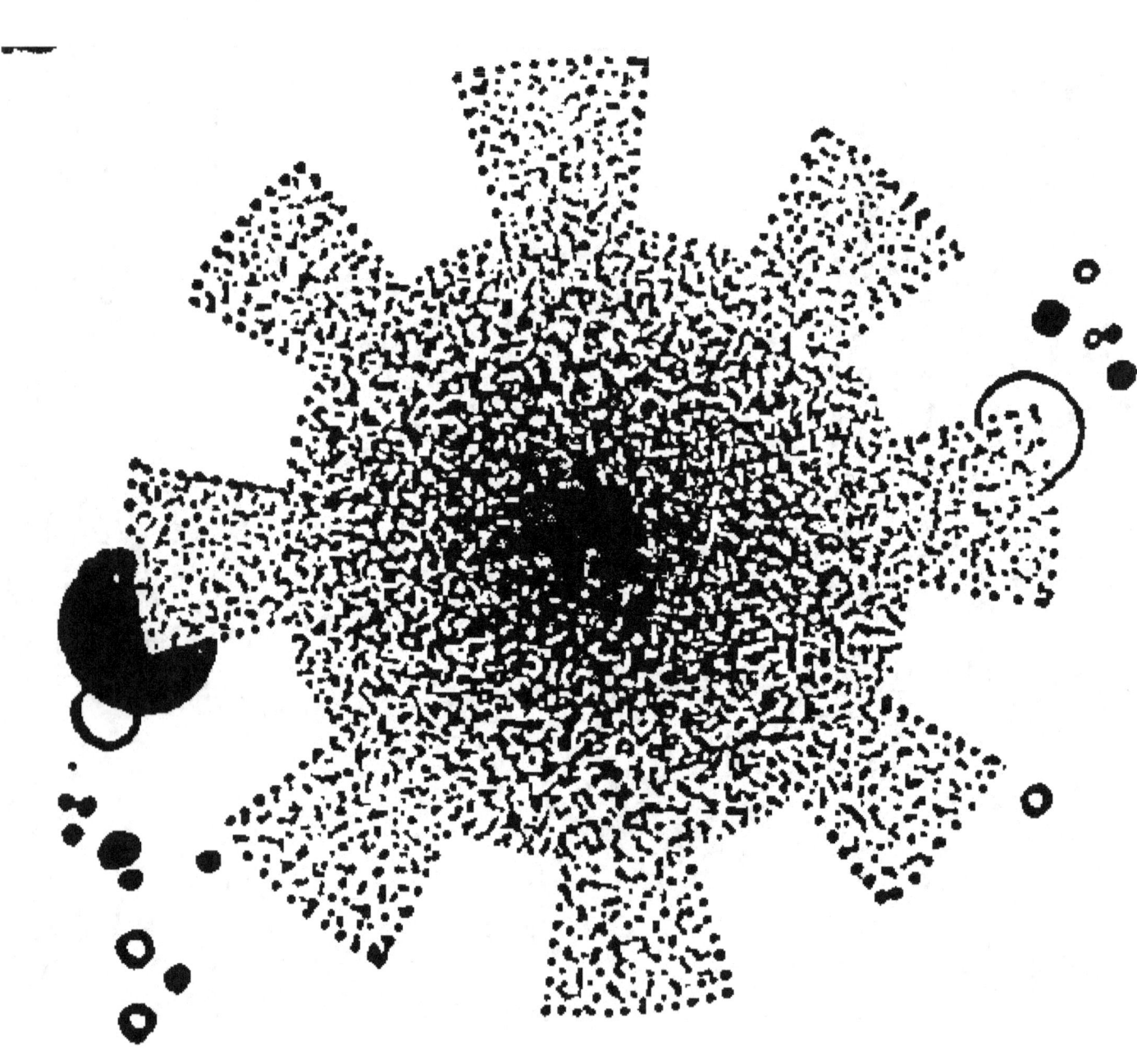

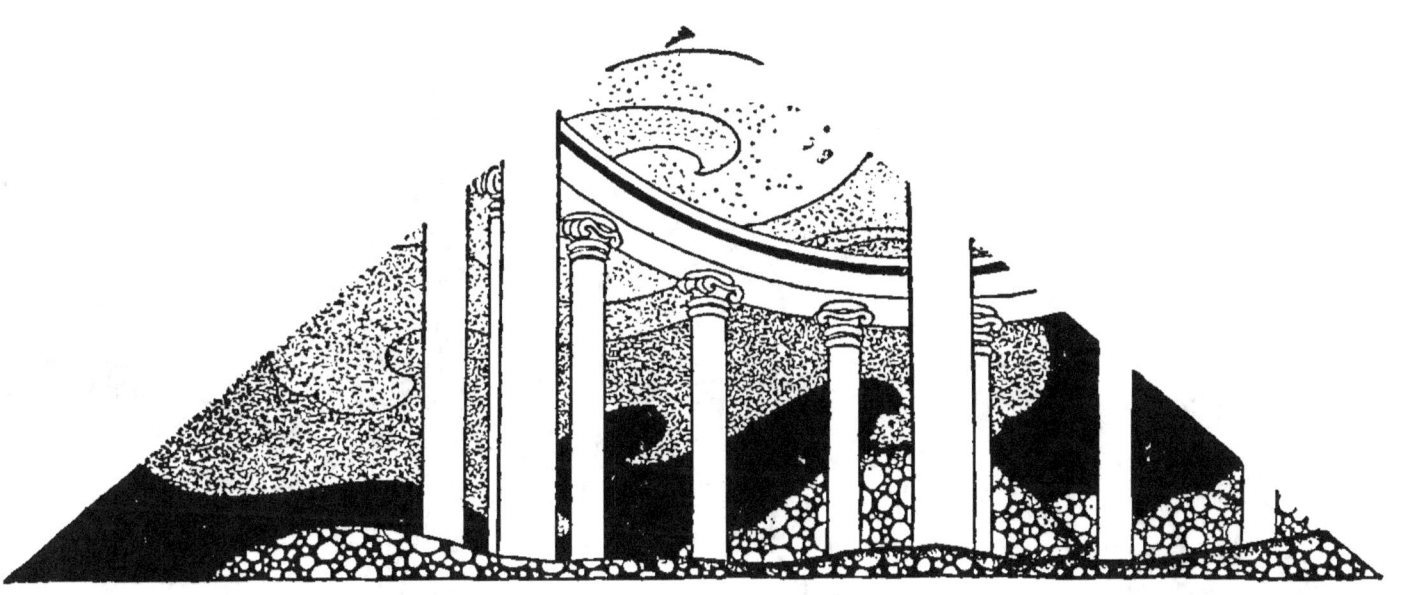

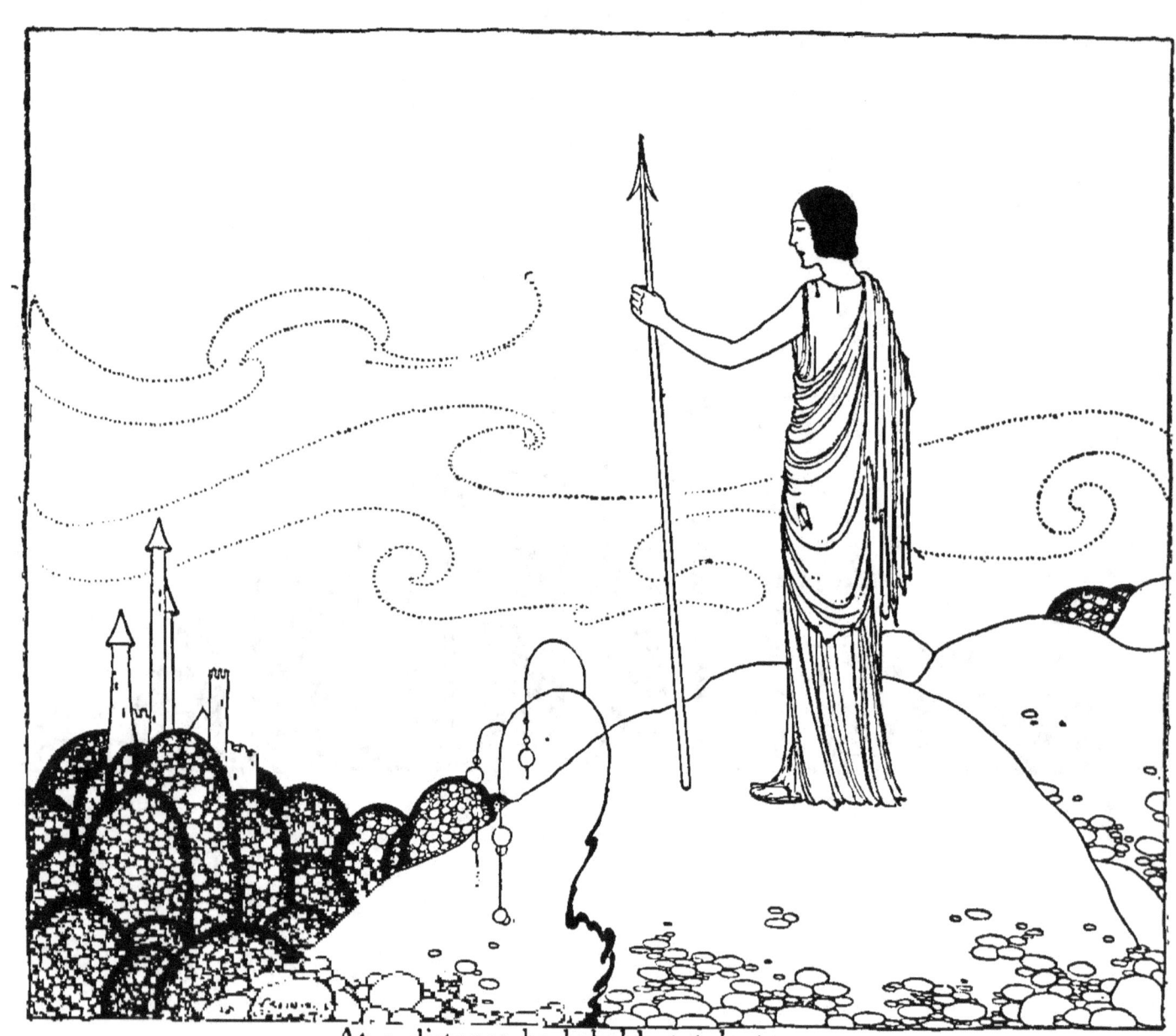
At a distance he beheld stately towers.

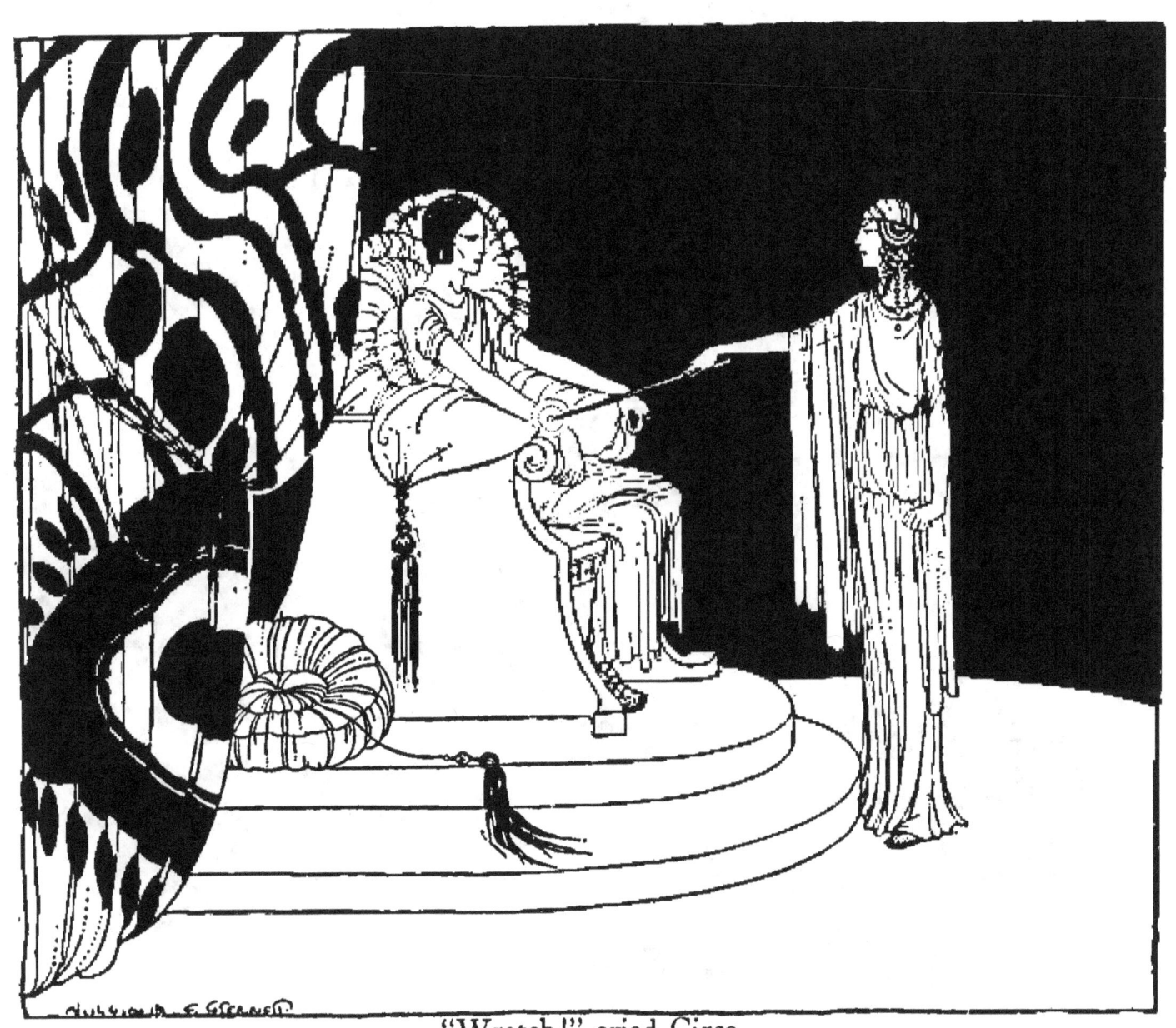

"Wretch!" cried Circe.

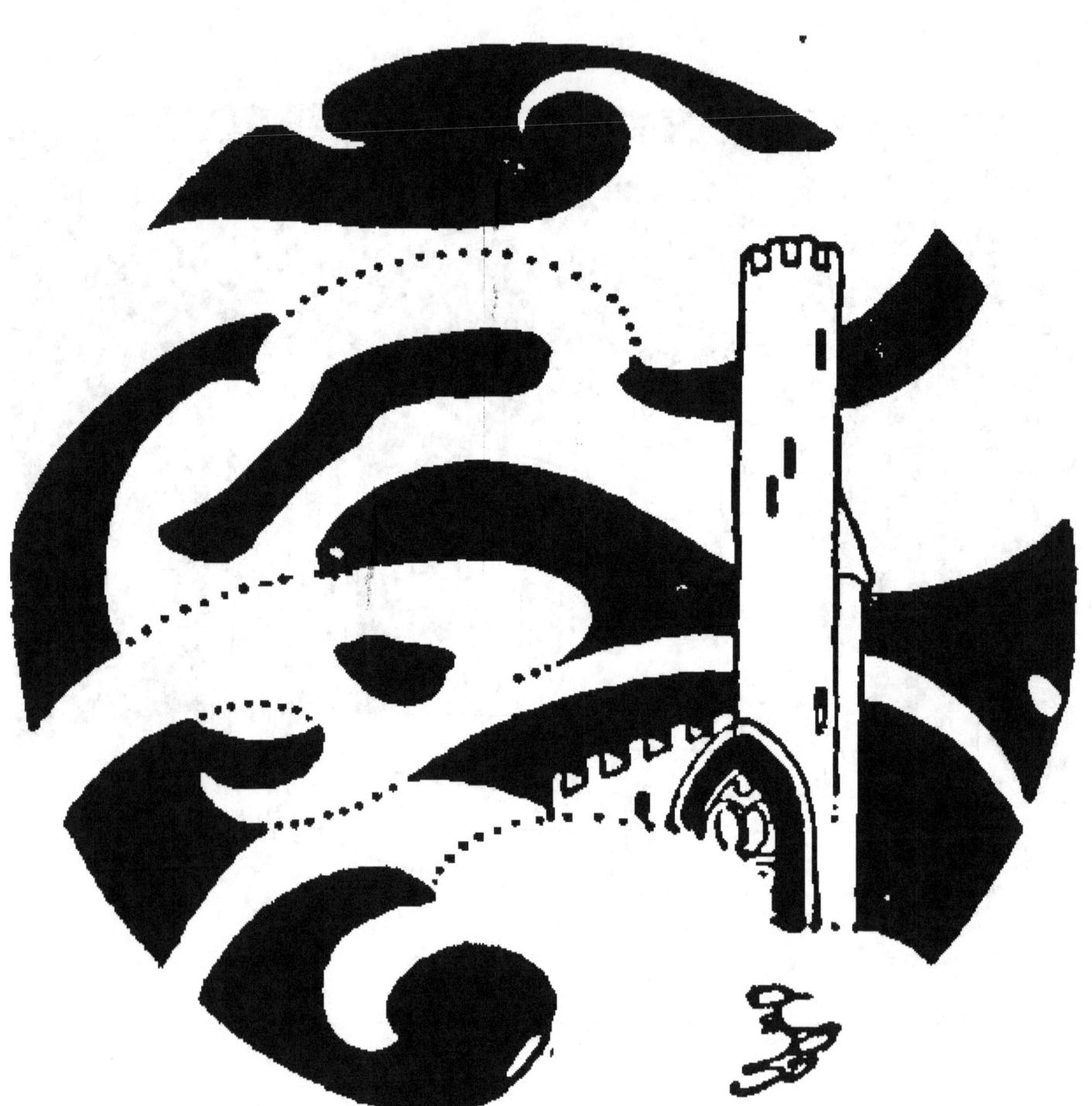

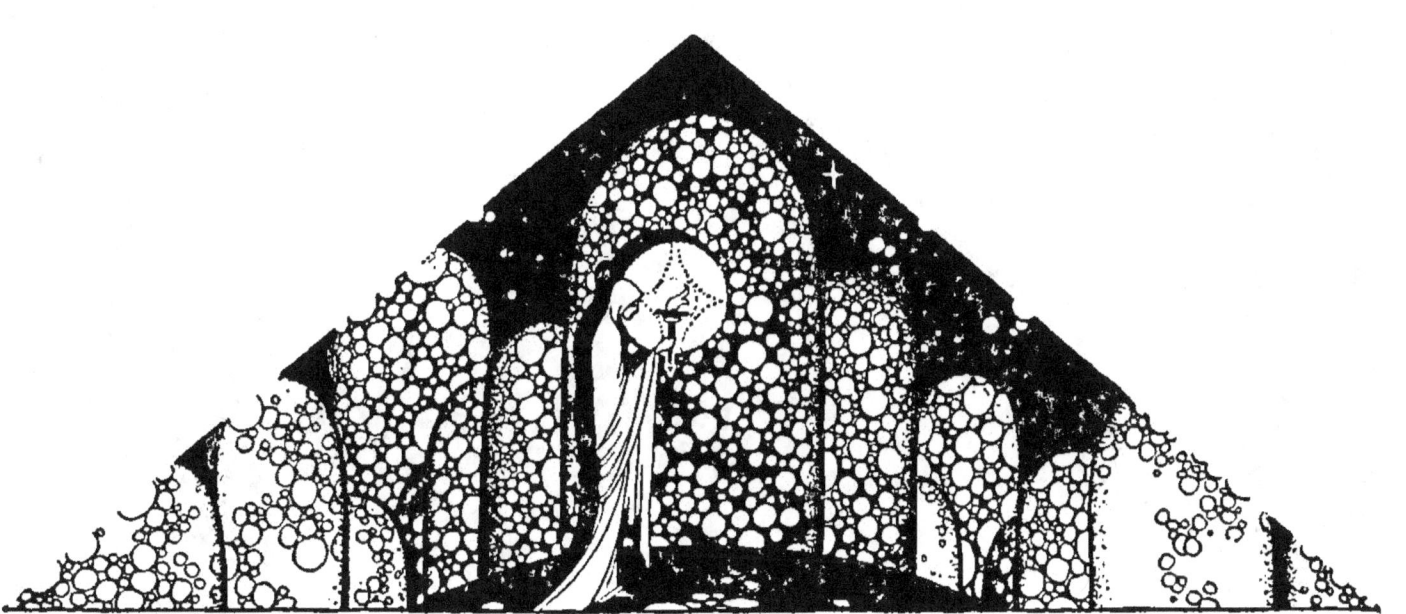

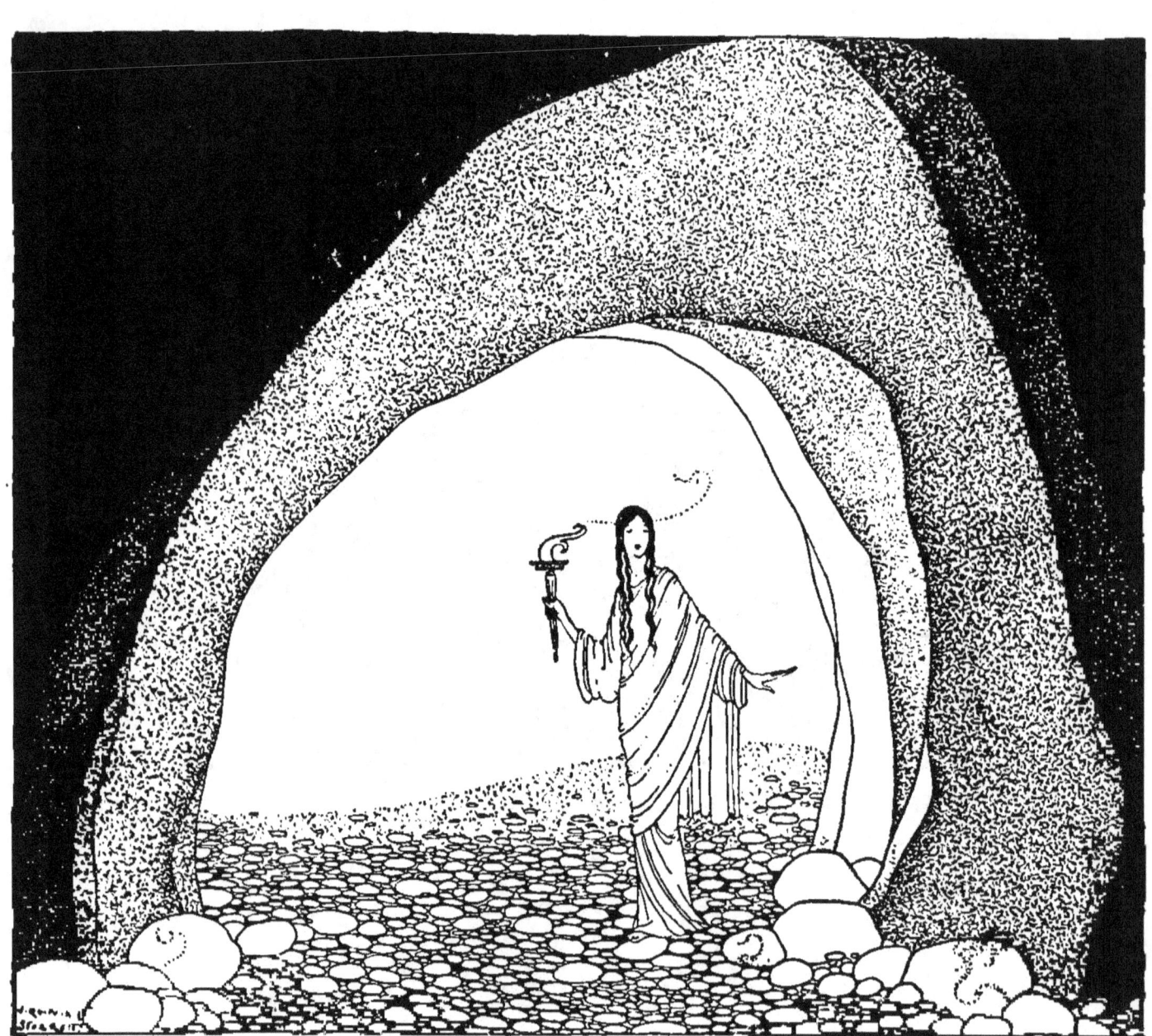

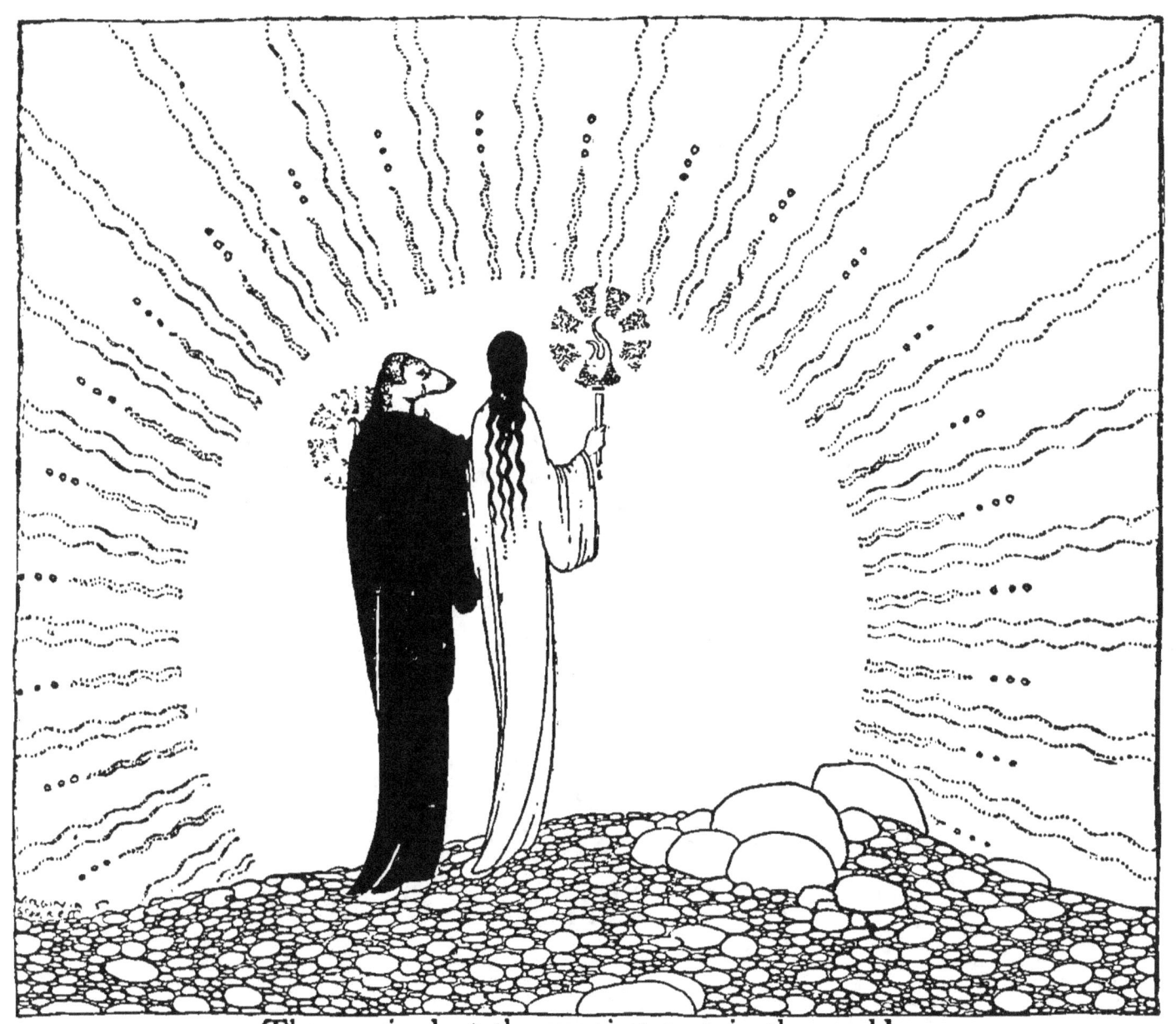
They arrived at the sunniest spot in the world.

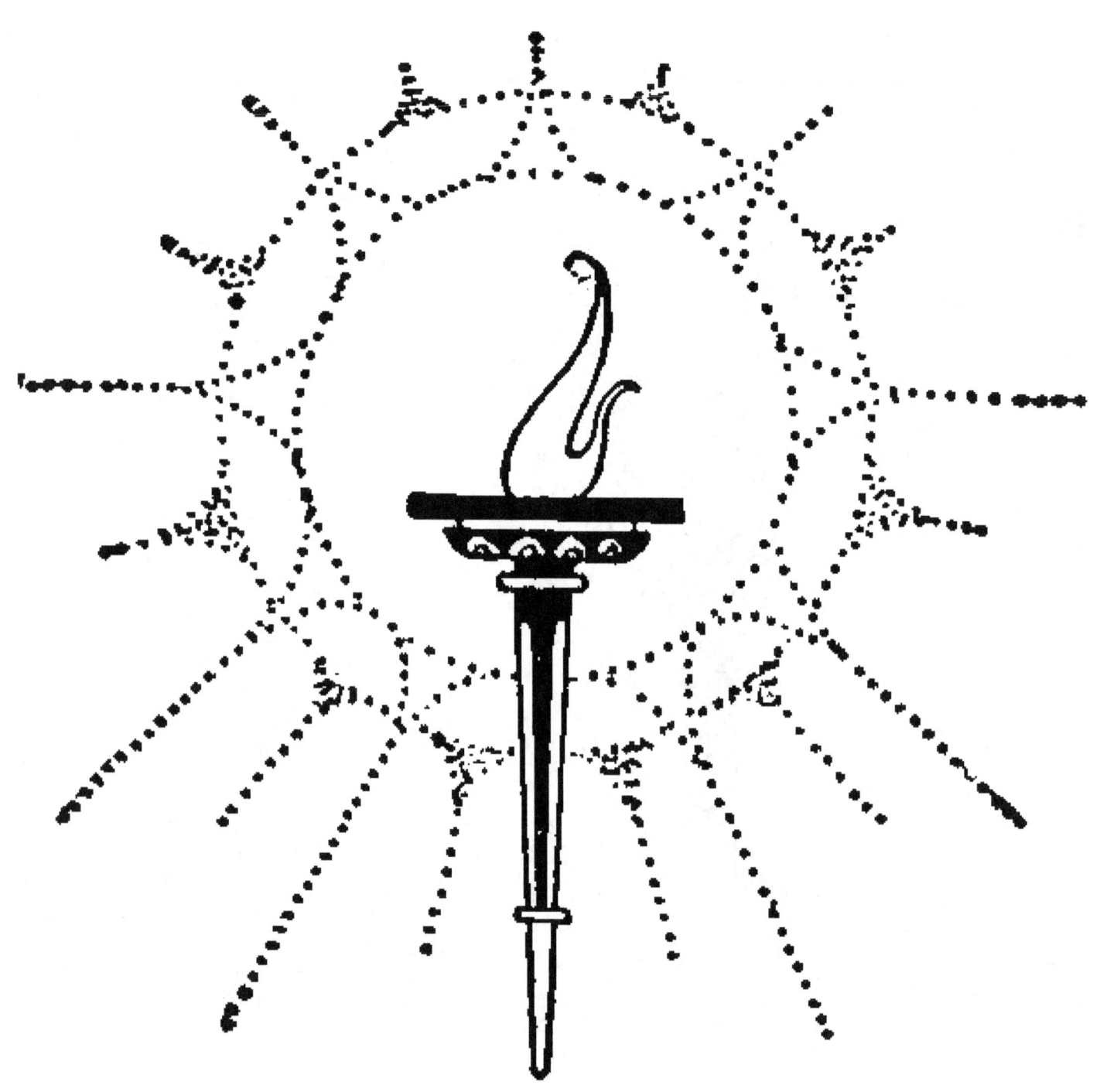

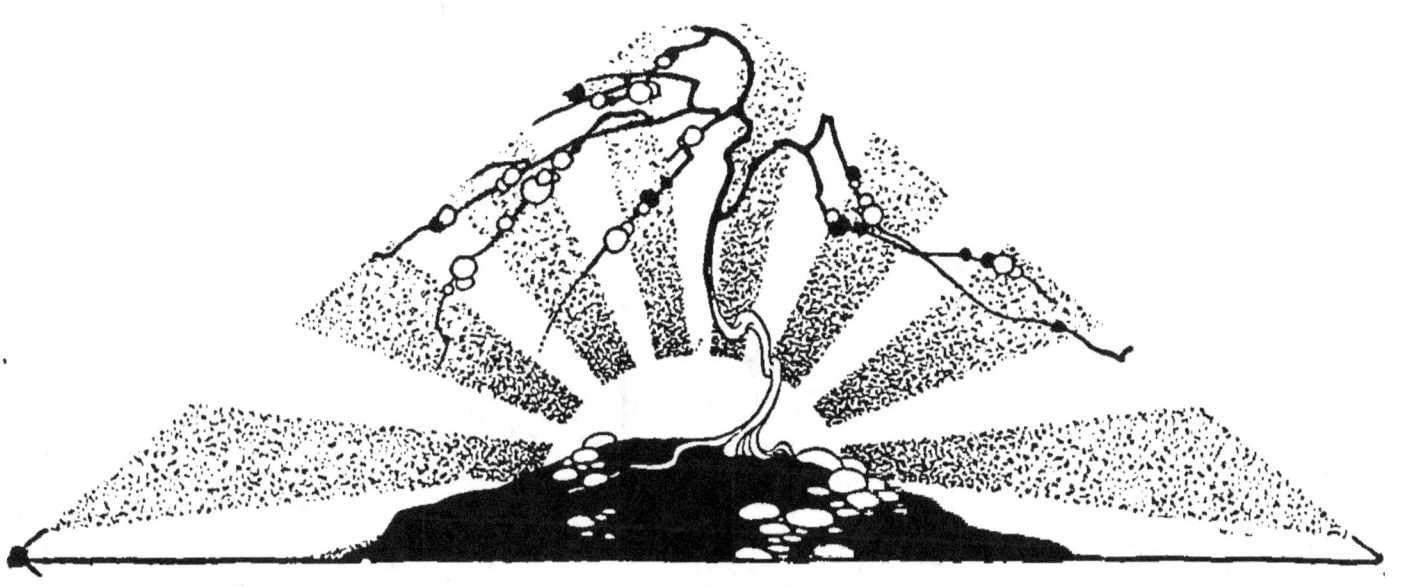

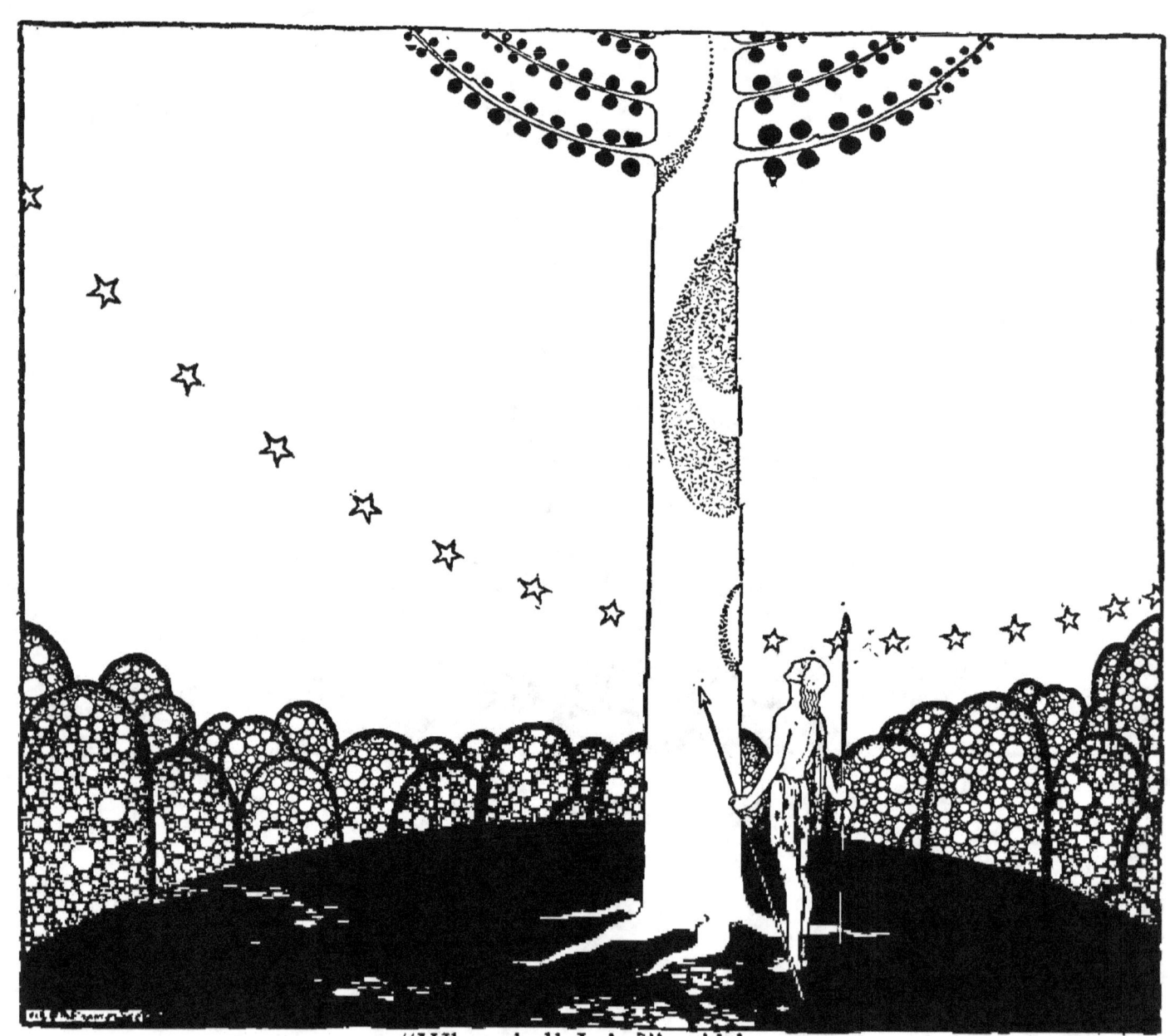
"What shall I do?" said he.

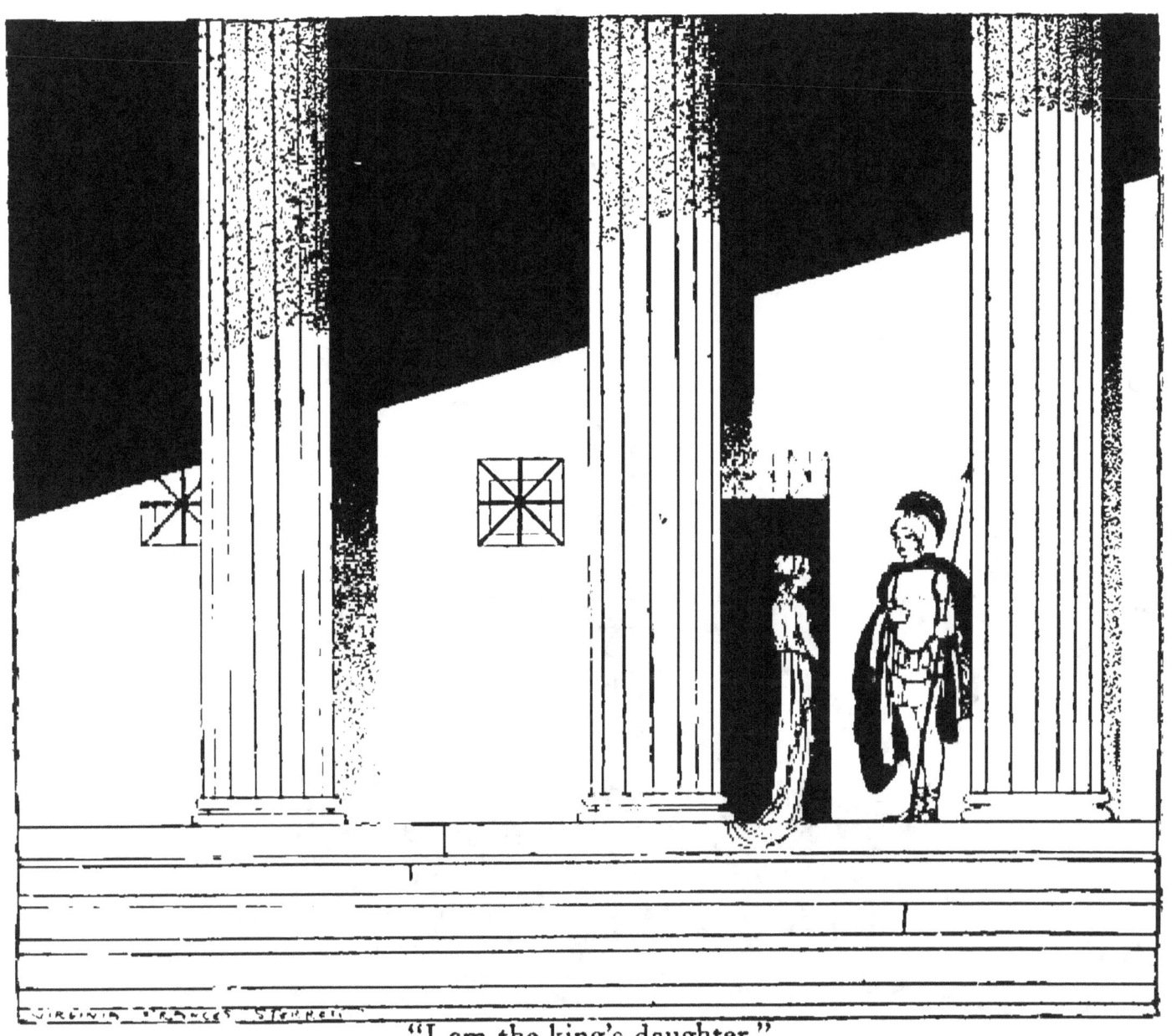
"I am the king's daughter."

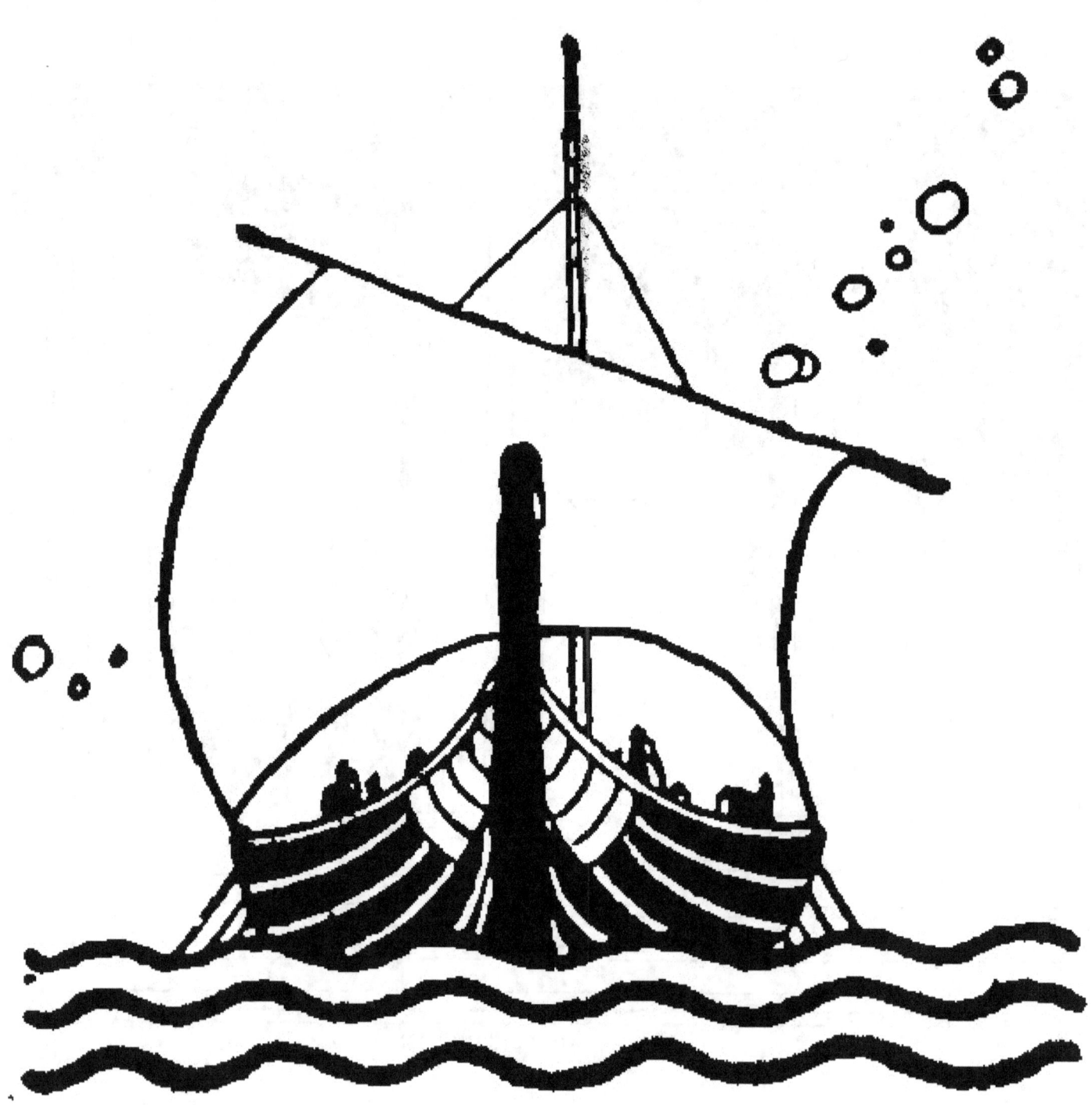

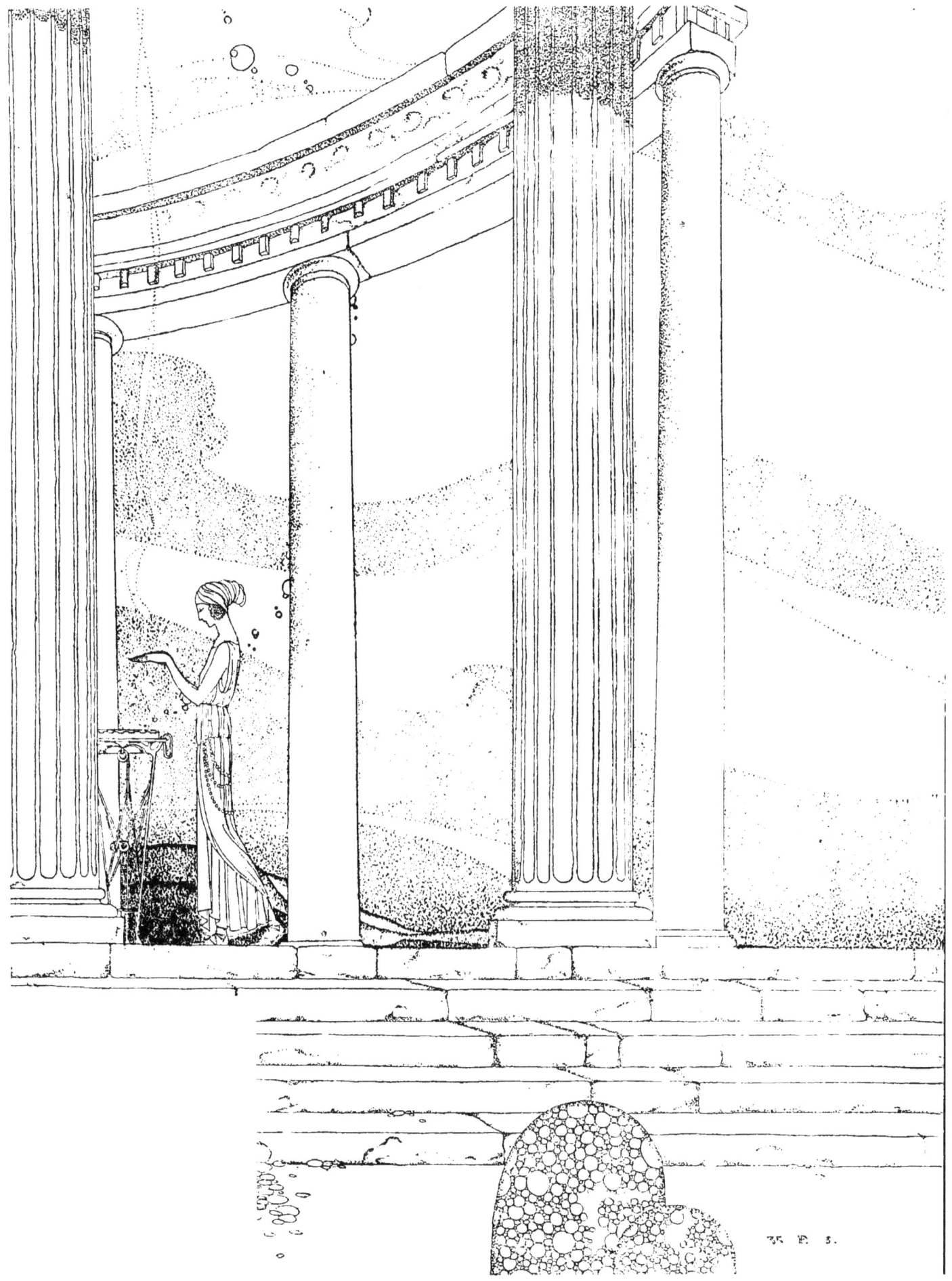

www.ingramcontent.com/pod-product-compliance
Lightning Source LLC
Chambersburg PA
CBHW082221220526
45470CB00010B/3255